Coming Through

Pam Rhodes is the main presenter of *Songs of Praise*. She is also a successful novelist whose titles include *With Hearts and Hymns and Voices*, *Ties That Bind*, *The Trespassers*, *Whispers* and *Letting Go*, and the author of an illustrated book of her favourite churches, *Living and Loved*. She lives in Hertfordshire.

PAM RHODES

Coming Through

TRUE STORIES OF HOPE
AND COURAGE

PAN BOOKS

First published 2001 by Sidgwick & Jackson

First published in paperback 2002 by Pan Books

This edition published 2007 by Pan Books
an imprint of Pan Macmillan Ltd
Pan Macmillan, 20 New Wharf Road, London N1 9RR
Basingstoke and Oxford
Associated companies throughout the world
www.panmacmillan.com

ISBN 978-0-330-45326-4

1 3 5 7 9 8 6 4 2

A CIP catalogue record for this book is available from
the British Library.

Printed and bound in Great Britain by
Mackays of Chatham plc, Chatham, Kent

CONTENTS

Introduction

'Good times don't build character.'

That's an old saying which has come to mind so often while I've been working on this book. It is a sad but true fact of life that it is sometimes only through the trauma of unexpected change that we find within ourselves the strengths and abilities we need to cope.

In *Coming Through* I have collected together the reminiscences of a very diverse group of people, each of whom has had to face an extraordinary challenge. They differ in age, situation, personality and nationality – and yet what they share is the experience of facing a physical or emotional difficulty which has required all their stamina, courage and resilience to bring them through. Some of them have been inadvertently caught up in headline stories familiar to us all – like Eileen Harrild, the gym teacher who was shot during the massacre at Dunblane. Others have had to cope with the sudden loss of someone or something they love – like the Honourable Mrs Frances Shand Kydd, who speaks with great insight and sensitivity about bereavement, having been through the pain of losing not only her daughter, Princess Diana, but her son, John, too. A few, such as the brilliant young jockey Declan Murphy, whose skull was crushed during a race at Haydock Park, have found their lives changed dramatically by a sudden diminishing of physical ability. Others have had to cope with shocking discoveries about those closest to them, leaving them to pick up the pieces once they realize that what they always trusted to be true is not at all what it seems.

A few of these people I have known and admired as friends for years. Others I have met along the way, occasionally, but certainly not always, through my role as the presenter of BBC Television's *Songs of Praise*. Several of them have found strength to face adversity through faith – mostly Christian, often less defined, more an acknowledgement of a power beyond themselves. For them, faith has plainly been a major factor in their struggle to 'come through'. However, these stories are not exclusive to 'believers' in any way. They resound with the power of the human heart and the soaring triumph of the spirit to overcome fear and pain, and face challenges square on. When the chips were down, all these people discovered the resources they needed from within, often surprising themselves as their previously untried strengths and skills made it possible for them to become more capable and confident in a way they had never dreamed they would need to be.

There is a roundness to each of these stories, where the teller is able to look back with hindsight, and share with the reader the benefit of the lessons in life learned on the way. Their stories are heart-warming, unbelievably moving and deeply inspiring – although often they make uncomfortable, even painful reading. These people speak in such an honest and heartfelt way about the difficult times they've come through, they each present to us a precious gift – that of hope. They came through. And as we face tough situations in our own lives, they give us hope that we can come through too.

Pam Rhodes

Angela

'The sun would have never set on the British Empire if previous generations had the gumption of the Ladies of Rylstone'

The Morning Star, Forth Worth, Texas

Rylstone is a tiny village in North Yorkshire. Blink and you'll miss it as you make your way up across the moors from Skipton. The village is little more than a cluster of cottages and houses stout enough to withstand the wind that whips across this chilly, wildly beautiful corner of England. There's a timeless quality here not just in the landscape, but also in the pace of life of a small out-of-the-way community. Here, neighbours really know and care about each other. They pop in and out with a helping hand and friendly gossip. They share school runs, and take turns playing host to each other's children. The men meet up in the pub, and the women help out at the church, probably starting off with the pre-school playgroup, then progressing on to the Women's Institute which once a month draws in ladies from Rylstone and the surrounding area for evenings of chat that open with the hymn 'Jerusalem', and end with tea and cakes. The average age of the WI members is probably nearer sixty than fifty, and their conversation is as likely to be about knitting patterns and cake recipes as world politics. But these practical, conservative ladies can certainly rise to a challenge. When one of their members found herself coping with the shocking and sudden loss of her husband through an aggressive form of lymphoma, the Women's Institute girls decided to rally round and raise a bit of money.

Their fund-raising idea was a simple one. They'd produce a calendar. And so they did! On the front of their 'Alternative' WI Calendar it says: 'When the ladies of Rylstone and District WI drop everything for their traditional crafts, "Jam and Jerusalem" will never be the same again!'

Well, that's certainly true! What they dropped were their clothes. What they raised is likely to amount to well over a million pounds in just two years!

When Angela and John Baker arrived in the village of Cracoe, not far from Rylstone, in 1974, it had far fewer residents than the 180 who live there today. The family moved in so that John could take up his post as the Assistant National Park Officer with the Yorkshire Dales National Park Authority. He had special responsibility for conservation and the National Park Warden Service and the Information Centres scattered around this area of outstanding natural beauty. This was a part of the country John knew well and had loved ever since he and his pals had cycled over there for outings when they were teenagers in Bradford.

There's nothing like having children to make friends when you've just moved to a new home. With Matthew only three years old, and Rachel aged six, Angela soon met up with other mums at the gate of the village school. Before long, she found herself taking charge of the Brownie Pack – and joining the Women's Institute.

'I'd never heard of the WI really,' she explains, 'when a lady in the village came and asked if I would like to go. I didn't know what to expect at all, but they made me so very welcome, and through becoming a member I got to know a lot more people who lived round about, because our club draws in ladies from a cluster of small villages, Rylstone, Cracoe Hetton, Bordley and Winterburn with Flasby. We meet on the first Thursday of every month, and there must have been as many as fifty there quite regularly when I first joined. Mind you, I was definitely one of the youngest at that time – and I've been a member now for almost thirty years. The average age today is probably about sixty – and at fifty-five, I'm probably *still* one of the youngest there! I suppose some people think of it as a fuddy-duddy organization, but that's not true at all. They try to keep up the traditional crafts, like embroidery and knitting. We have talks from some fascinating speakers, and there's always a good supper. It's an entertaining evening out. We always begin by singing "Jerusalem", because that is the Women's Institute hymn. Then we sort out any business, including information about what's coming up – then the speaker, supper, and home about half past nine.'

Once John and Angela's children had grown up and flown the nest, they found time to enjoy each other's company again. 'We just loved doing things together,' says Angela. 'We knew the kids were happy and doing what they wanted, so we decided to do some of the things we'd always talked about. We loved our holidays, maybe somewhere warm where we could just sit together by the sea, reading books. And we had some wonderful adventure holidays too. John had a great sense of humour, and always made me laugh. I suppose that most of all, we felt safe with each other – so much so that we didn't need to say anything sometimes, because we just knew what the other was thinking. Every now and then, we'd even come out with the same thing at the same time – that's how much in tune we were.'

They'd met when Angela was just eighteen, and running a travel bureau in the Students' Union office of Sheffield University. When John came in with three student friends to book a holiday in Yugoslavia, Angela glanced across at him, and thought, 'Mmmm, he looks a bit of all right!' His friends were quite chatty, but John was obviously the shy one – and from the form he filled in for the holiday, Angela learned not just that he was a sociology student, but where he lived, and even his date of birth. They left, and she wondered if that would be the last she saw of him, especially when the lads popped in later to find out if their tickets had arrived, and John wasn't with them.

A big dance was coming up at the university, and when John's friends asked Angela if she was going, she said she was without mentioning that she would probably be there on her own. 'Then something wonderful happened! At exactly five to five (and I can be precise about this momentous occasion because it was just as *Crackerjack* was starting) John rang up and asked me to be his partner at the dance. Would I?! We were engaged by graduation day, and married the year after, in 1966.'

Long after their own wedding, Angela took on a job where she became an important part of other people's marriages – as the local registrar. 'I enjoyed marrying people because it was such a happy day for them. I especially loved registering the babies because I always had a cuddle, and if they were crying, I used to get them to be quiet and go to sleep. The mums said I had a knack with them. And I took special care when people came in to register deaths, because I realized how difficult it was to come in and tell me about the death of someone they had loved for a long time. I tried to make it easier for them, and took time to listen if they simply wanted to talk. I knew they dreaded coming in to see the registrar on such a sad occasion, and often they said that it hadn't been half as bad as they thought it would be. So I was glad to think that through my job, I had helped people at a very distressing time –

and I had such a lot of happy memories too. I think that probably made me appreciate John even more. After doing the weddings on a Saturday, John would be waiting for me, and I used to think that no one had a husband as wonderful as mine. We used to hold hands everywhere we went, and at night we'd sit on the settee together cuddled up. We were big softies really.'

John died on 22 July 1998. He was 54 years old.

'He was a really fit man, six foot tall, and twelve stone — someone who enjoyed running, and never went to the doctor's. The first inkling I had that he was ill was when he had a pain in his stomach on Christmas Eve '97. For the first time in years, he was concerned enough to go to the doctor that day. He was told there wasn't too much to worry about — perhaps it was a hernia? Tests could be done after Christmas.

'By February, I began to notice that he looked a little older, and was more tired — but it was when he started having violent night sweats that he went to the doctor again. After blood tests and a visit to the specialist, we were soon told that they had found a growth in his small intestine about the size of a grapefruit. He had a very aggressive form of lymphoma. They operated straight away, but they couldn't take all the growth out because it was attached to his abdominal wall. Within three weeks, it had grown again to the size of an aubergine. He was very weak, but he was fighting! He was so brave, determined not to let it beat him.

'For the next five months, he was mostly at home — and in that time, I think we had five good days when he felt up to doing something. He was plainly very ill, mostly laid low with high temperatures.

'But it's at times like that when you really recognize how wonderful your friends are. The girls I'd first met through the Women's Institute had become my closest friends, and they were absolutely fantastic. When John was at home, three of them took it in turns to sleep at our house so that they could be there for John, and I could get a bit of rest. It's very frightening, nursing someone you love who is very ill — and knowing there was someone else in the house with me was such a comfort.

'It was Trish Stewart who first brought up the idea of a rather different sort of calendar. We were all at the WI one night when we were asked if we had any nice photographs for the Women's Institute calendar. We knew exactly what they were looking for — beautiful sunsets or snow scenes, waterfalls and village ponds — it was the same sort of thing every year. Then Trish turned to me and said, "You know, we could do our own version, with us doing the traditional crafts of the WI but in the style of a Pirelli calendar!" I remember laughing and agreeing with her, but not taking it very seriously. Then I went home and told John that Trish had suggested we should star in our own "Alternative WI Calendar" in the nude — he laughed out loud!

'But not long after that, as John became very ill, he was really touched when a group of friends did a walk of the Three Peaks, twenty-six miles long, and raised two thousand pounds for the ward in Leeds where he was being treated. It was then that Trish brought the idea up again. He grinned, and said, "Trish, who in their right mind's going to take their clothes off?" She explained that we could do it really tastefully, so it wasn't smutty at all. "We could raise money for the Leukemia Research Fund, and if we sell them at about £5 each, we might even be lucky enough to sell a thousand copies — and that would be a lot of money." And then she teased John, because they always had a good banter between them. "And John, because you're poorly, you can come and watch!" I remember his face so clearly as he laughed with her, before he said more seriously, "You'll never do it." And the saddest thing is that he didn't live long enough to know that we did.'

John died in July. Angela knew that the one thing above all else that he would have liked to do was to raise money to help prevent other families having to cope with an illness like his. By September, Trish had gathered together eleven volunteers from among the WI friends who had known John to be featured in photographs from January to November – with a festive group shot as the crowning glory for December. Only one Calendar Girl was recruited from outside the WI members. Ros Fawcett, who lives in Cracoe, was in the pub on the evening when the girls were deciding who should pose for which month, and what traditional craft each month should feature. Ros had been a great support to Angela and John during his illness – and before she knew it, she was signing up for the WI and taking on the role of Miss November.

The question of who would take the photos was quickly settled. Miss July, Linda, and her husband, Terry, were both artists – and Terry had an excellent eye for the setting up, lighting and taking of photographs. Their house would provide a range of perfect back-drops for a variety of poses, and all the girls agreed that there would be no embarrassment at the thought of taking off their clothes providing they could keep dressing gowns on while Terry set up the shot and positioned the camera, then left the room so that Linda could click the shutter. First to pose was Moira, who was so nervous at the thought of becoming Miss May that she decided it would be best to get her session over first. Everything went according to plan. Moira kept on her dressing gown as Terry set up the shot – and then once he left the room, she graciously arranged a lovely display of flowers in an elegant vase which hid her blushes, but not the fact that she was absolutely starkers except for a string of pearls! But 'clicking the shutter' was not quite the straightforward business the girls thought it would be. When things didn't go quite as planned, Linda was shouting through the door, 'Oh Terry, this has happened . . . What should I try here? What do you think I should do about that?'

In the end, Angela said, 'For goodness sake, just let Terry take it! He can't see anything, so let him get on with it!' After a little hesitation, Moira agreed – and they were on their way. Angela took her turn next, reassuring those who were a bit nervous of Terry, rather than Linda, actually taking their photographs, by sitting down at the piano, apparently bashing out an enthusiastic rendering of "Jerusalem" with her back to the camera, but plainly without a stitch on. 'I just thought, if I could do it, they all could. Terry is our friend, and we knew he was very discreet. If we were going to do it, we had to get on with it, and do it right.'

Before long, all eleven months up to November were safely in the can, which left the hardest set-up of all – December, in which all eleven girls, complete with Santa hats, carol sheets and nothing more than big smiles, posed alongside mince pies and mulled wine. 'Can you imagine?' says Angela with a grin. 'Eleven women, all with their bits and pieces to be hidden! I think Terry took about three rolls of film, and there was only one shot that was decent.'

Every photograph had two things in common. The first was the string of pearls which each model wore around their neck. 'This was because,' explains Angela, 'in the early days of the WI, the ladies used to wear tweed skirts, twin sets and pearls. We thought we'd take off everything else – but leave the pearls.'

And secondly, where all the photos were given a traditional sepia finish, the only splash of colour on each month's picture is a bright yellow sunflower. This was decided upon because of John's own fondness for sunflowers, especially as so many of his get well soon cards in hospital featured the cheerful flowers. 'We thought that sunflowers looked happy, as if they were always smiling at you,' says Angela. 'After John came out of hospital, our daughter-in-law, Georgina, who is also Linda and Terry's daughter, arrived with a packet of sunflower seeds. She had read on the back that if they were planted in spring, they would be in bloom in August and

September, which should have been when John had finished his chemotherapy and would be in remission. So we started the seeds off, then gave them to all our friends asking if they would grow them for John. We gave about one hundred away, and they all grew beautifully in other people's gardens. Sadly, though, John didn't live long enough to see them – but from that time on, sunflowers always made us think of him. Every house I went to seemed to have a flower growing just for him. It was lovely – so it felt right when Terry suggested that including a bright yellow flower on each page of the calendar would make it special for John.'

Planning the calendar was one thing. The reality of seeing the finished article, which is the picture of elegance with its sepia-toned photos, tongue-in-cheek captions, and moving tribute to John on the back, surprised and delighted the girls of the Rylstone WI. As Angela puts it, 'I just thought, heck, that's brilliant!' But what would the rather more staid, national Women's Institute organization make of such a very 'alternative' WI calendar, without a village pond or snow scene in sight?

'They were fantastic from the very start. We went with our mock-up to the head office in London to ask for their blessing – and without reservation, they gave it. The next hurdle was to visit the national headquarters of the Leukemia Research Fund to see if they agreed that the calendar could be used to raise money for them. I remember there were two ladies there, our local fund organizer, Jennifer, and their PR man, Andrew, who was only young. I think we were all old enough to be his mum, really – and there we were, sitting round this table, showing him pictures of ourselves with no clothes on! His reaction was great. He just said it was wonderful, and that he didn't think we realized just what we'd got here. And how very right he was!

'Because we'd managed to get local sponsorship to cover our production costs, when we got to the printing, we thought hard about how many copies we might possibly sell. Dare we go for a thousand? We could sell to our family and friends, and then each take twenty calendars, to try and distribute them on a sale or return basis. And as Trish said, she could always moisten down any that were left, and make them into brickets for the fire during the winter months!

'At that point, Jennings, the local brewery, came on board after we asked if we could have a small launch party on 12 April 1999, at our local pub, The Devonshire Arms. Their PR man suggested that we should send out a photo and press release to all the major newspapers – so we did. No one was more surprised than us at their reaction. That launch day is something I will just never ever forget. Our little pub in the tiny village of Cracoe was packed with cameramen and microphones, radio reporters, journalists and photographers. By lunch-time, I was on local television. At six o'clock, we made the BBC National News – and at five o'clock the next morning we were all up early to make an appearance on GMTV. It was unbelievable – we were just swept along with it. It was so exciting!'

Their initial run of one thousand calendars, which they had worried so much about selling, disappeared in a matter of days. The brewers, Jennings, had been tremendously supportive by organizing mail order deliveries for them up to end of October – but as they got busier with their own orders in the run-up to Christmas, the calendars landed in Angela's garage, where a dedicated band of people helped every day to reply to the hundreds of request letters which arrived by the sackful. Envelopes were addressed, calendars popped in, sealed up and taken to the post office at breakneck speed. By the turn of the Millennium, the start of year 2000, 88,000 calendars had been sold – all for £5 each.

'I think,' says Angela, 'the whole idea that "ladies of a certain age" like us should take their clothes off in a tasteful way to raise money for an excellent cause just caught everyone's imagination. We got so many letters from fellow members of the WI saying that our calendar was just what had been needed for years to rid the organization of its unwarranted stuffy image. They said things like, "What a shame I didn't think of it. I'd have loved to have been part of the whole thing!" It was all so encouraging. But mostly other women simply said, "Well done for portraying our age group in such a positive way. You've proved that you don't have to be six foot tall, stick thin, and under twenty to be attractive and interesting.' Obviously the press thought that too, because we were then invited by the national magazine, *Woman's Journal*, to spend three days at London's Fashion Week as models in a big fashion show at the Savoy Hotel. We had to keep pinching ourselves to be sure it was really happening to *us*, eleven members of the WI from Rylstone, Yorkshire! There we all were – tall, medium, short – on the catwalk wearing the same clothes as those lovely young models with beautiful bodies – and believe it or not, the whole place erupted with applause when we made our first appearance. We all came off crying our eyes out. It was amazing, absolutely amazing! And the last time we stepped on to that stage, we all walked down with sunflowers, just to remind ourselves and everyone else what it was all about. I just thought, John would have been so proud—

'Then came another wonderful day when we were all invited to the 'Woman of the Year' ceremony in London. It was brilliant, because we were being filmed for a BBC documentary at the time, so as everyone was lining up to be announced, we had to make our appearance *twice* for the cameras. It was a terrific feeling, and so unexpected. Then later we were invited along to another glittering occasion, the Oldies Dinner, when we were presented with an award by Terry Wogan, for The Under Exposure of the Year. I remember looking out on a sea of stars – and there they were clapping us. We couldn't believe it!'

The girls have had frantically busy months ever since, packed with talks to WI groups and calendar signings in stores and county shows, where they always wear their agreed 'uniform' of black dress, pearls and a bright yellow sunflower. 'We just thought we'd all got a little black dress in the wardrobe – and it shows the sunflower off a treat!

'We even took two calendars along to Buckingham Palace, because both the Queen and the Queen Mother are members of the Sandringham branch of the Women's Institute. We were thrilled when we received letters from them both saying thank you very much.

'I think in a way the hardest part of all this was telling my Mum and Dad right at the start. They're both in their eighties now, and John was like a son to them, so his death was a great loss. I remember saying to Mum that we were appearing in a calendar, and she said, "That's a good idea." And then I had to tell her that we'd got no clothes on, and she said, "Oh, dear, do you think that's right?" But when she and Dad actually saw the calendar, they really loved it – and best of all, they thought John would have loved it too.'

But taking the British Isles by storm has been just the start. On 23 January 2000, news of the calendar hit the *New York Times*. TV people poured over from America, including the producer of the coast to coast '20/20 Show' presented by Barbara Walters. Their appearance on that show started an unprecedented interest across the United States, where the Rylstone Calendar Girls were hailed as 'The UK's hottest female ensemble since the Spice Girls!' Before long, they had found a publisher in the States who brought out a version of their calendar which began on I June 2000, shortly after the American celebration of Mothering Sunday. 'It just felt right that the calendar should begin on that date, because it would have been John's birthday. And so far, they've made a million dollars, with another calendar beginning at the start of the year 2001. And more than that, a feature film is being made about our story — can you believe that? They're even talking about there being a Royal premiere, one here in Britain, and another in America. We've been closely involved in the writing of the script, so we know it's been very sensitively done, and really captures the spirit of why we did the calendar in the first place. Mind you, we couldn't possibly have imagined then, as we sat in the pub in Cracoe making our initial plans, that it would lead to everything which has happened to us since!

'Before all this began, none of us were really the types to push ourselves forward — even giving the vote of thanks at a WI meeting would have been an ordeal for some of the girls — but this whole experience has given us such a lot of confidence. The hardest part for me sometimes is to stop myself crying. I'm so overwhelmed by the kindness and enthusiasm of the people I meet. It's incredibly moving at times.

'Often I get letters from total strangers saying that John must have been a wonderful man, and how proud he would have been of what we're doing, and the money we've raised. Sometimes they've had friends or relatives themselves who have died from leukemia, so our effort has particular meaning for them. I remember talking to the lady on the switchboard of the Leukemia Lymphoma Society of America one day, because we are sharing the royalties of the American calendar with them. She asked if I was one of the ladies who had done the calendar, and I said I was, and that John had been my husband. She said, "Well, I reckon you'll make a million, and just think — that might be the million they are waiting for to make a breakthrough in this terrible disease." I've thought about that often since, because I feel it might be true. I have to believe there's a reason why John had to die. He didn't lose his life for nothing. Just think what he's achieved. That would have meant so much to him.

'And of course, he knew about the idea of making a calendar. He laughed with us about it — even said we'd never do it! He'd be so thrilled now, to know that all this money has been raised so that other people may not suffer in the future as he did.'

It's clear that the closeness of this small group of women friends has helped Angela cope with the grief of losing her much-loved husband. The experience has changed their lives for ever — yet they are still close, still attend WI meetings, and are still fiercely loyal to one another even though they've had their moments of disagreement over the months since the publication of the calendar. But however exciting and challenging life has become for Angela, she, like any widow, goes back to a house which seems dreadfully empty without John. 'I suppose I relied on him so much, and he was always there to give me encouragement, advice, or just to talk things over. I used to tell him everything, my innermost thoughts — and I've missed that so much. I've had to learn how to run the house, pay the bills and do the garden. Worst of all is being in the house alone overnight because I hate the dark. I just feel, though, that he's there giving me the strength to get through this. Sometimes, because of the calendar, I've had to give talks, and I've thought, I can't, I just can't get up on the stage and do this — but I've managed, and it's almost as if he's there with me, wanting me to do well. I've become so much stronger through it all.

'I remember meeting a Church of England minister some time ago, who believed in the healing power of faith. He came to us, and we all prayed together. Then he said that I had a wonderful garden full of beautiful wild birds — and he told me not to forget that the spirit is in the birds. I've thought of that often since John died, especially when I'm feeling sad and down. I think back to Sunday mornings when we used to have tea in bed together and look out at the birds in the garden — only I can't bear to do that alone now, because it is too painful a memory, so I come downstairs and have a cup of tea on my own in the kitchen. Then I began to notice the robin. He sits on the garage wall right outside the window, looking at me. Sometimes he's even come on to the window ledge and flapped, as if he's saying "I'd really like to be in there with you, but I can't be." Sometimes he waits in the tree for me to come home so that as soon as he sees me, he flies down. He was with me all winter, and then throughout the summer too — and you don't usually see robins in the summer, do you?

'I think of what that minister said about the spirit being birds. I remember how John and I used to watch the birds together. And I feel the comfort that little bird brings me, almost as if John is there too. I sense he's always close, keeping watch over me, encouraging me with everything the calendar has achieved because I know it would bring him a great deal of pride and pleasure. It will never bring him back — but it's wonderful to know that even though he lost his own life, he has contributed so much to the future health of countless other people around the world.'

Steve

In the hushed, twilight world of professional snooker, where competition is intense and huge winnings are at stake, the name of Steve Sanders is up among the very best. In the mid-seventies, he was part of the golden quartet of newcomers to the sport that included Steve Davis, Jimmy White and Tony Meo. By the late eighties, he was the European Masters Champion. He had his own television series, played snooker with Prince Charles, and was the envy of many for his fame and good fortune.

Only a few years later, Steve was homeless, drunk, violent and sleeping rough on the beach at Bournemouth. This is his story.

Steve was still at junior school when a friend of his father's gave him an old six-foot snooker table complete with a few marbles and a motley selection of odd balls. By the time he was twelve and had moved up to secondary school, a pal of his invited him along for a proper game of snooker at the local billiard hall. That was it. He was hooked. Within a year his potential was being noticed, and from the age of fourteen he was regularly playing truant from school so he could travel up to London for visits to snooker clubs at which top professionals like Alex Higgins, John Virgo and Patsy Fagan played. It didn't take those professionals long to realize that young Steve Sanders would make them work to win a match against him. He was fifteen years old, and already earmarked for stardom in the cut-throat world of snooker.

One of the managers of top players at that time took Steve under his wing, and entered him into a whole series of amateur competitions which he easily won. Articles about him started appearing first in leading snooker magazines, then in the general press – and before long television beckoned too. By the age of sixteen, the BBC had already made a documentary programme about the young man who was attracting a great deal of attention and admiration during their popular transmissions of snooker games. A year younger than Steve Davis, and a contemporary of other up-and-coming youngsters like Jimmy White and Tony Meo, Steve Sanders' star shone brightly. This was a beguiling world in which money, influence, friends, booze and flashy cars came easy – a long way from his experience of growing up in a Salvation Army family and being a schoolboy.

'I was getting plenty of attention from the general public,' says Steve, 'and that acknowledgement was like a round of applause, which I had never experienced before. In school, I was always picked on, especially by the teachers, who said I was useless. I remember when I was fifteen and had officially left school, one particular teacher told the class coming up for their last year that whatever they did, they must make sure they didn't end up like Steve Sanders, because all I did was play snooker and miss school, and I'd never get anywhere in life! The funny thing was that all the kids who were moving up to that year knew me because I was regularly appearing on television then. That teacher had an old red car, and years later when I was twenty and earning about a thousand pounds a week, I went past the school in my Jaguar, and saw him at the traffic lights in his old broken-down car. I couldn't resist looking out of the window to say hello. He asked me if I was all right, and I said, "I'm doing a lot better than you. You've still got that ropey car!" '

Once Steve had turned professional, he was making big money not just from tournaments and television, but also by playing the circuit of holiday camps like Butlins, Pontin's and Warners along with other top players like Ray Reardon and Stephen Hendry. Appearances by celebrity snooker pros were a big draw, and the rewards for the players were generous not just in terms of money, but in recognition, acclaim and the high life. 'It was unbelievable,' says Steve. 'I was spending twenty-pound notes as if there was no tomorrow, mixing with celebrities who were getting drunk and partying with the top sort of dolly birds, if you know what I mean. I thought it was great. It was all I wanted. It was like living a life of royalty. Everything was done for me. I've never had so much attention. I had a driver to take me to every tournament. I'd just click my fingers and a drink would be put in my hand. I could have a different girl for every night of the week, if I wanted it. I remember George Jackson and Patsy Fagan coming into the bar one day when I had a cigarette in one hand and a pint of lager in the other. They said, "What on earth do you think you're doing?" "I'm just smoking and having a drink. You smoke and drink!" As I was only eighteen then, they were really worried about me. I can remember them saying that I should put the ciggies and booze down because one day they would ruin my life. I just laughed at them. In fact, I was drinking quite a lot by then, probably because of the people I was mixing with. It felt like being part of a big social club. I thought it wasn't really affecting me, even when I started to hit the shorts.'

One night while he was playing snooker, he caught the eye of a girl at the bar. Her name was Kim — and at the age of twenty, probably 'hoping for a bit of security to run back to if everything went wrong', Steve and Kim were married. But his lifestyle didn't change, even when their daughter, Emma, was born on 4 April

1981. Steve went on travelling, drinking and socializing as if neither his wife nor his daughter had any importance for him. Three years later, the marriage simply fell apart.

'In fact, I felt quite gutted about that, but I just carried on, mixing with celebrities, having a good time. Best of all, I was playing really well, creeping up the ladder on the European circuit until, by the time I was twenty-six, I was ranked second seed in Europe.'

In 1987, Steve got an official letter asking if he would help with The Prince's Trust, which encourages young people within their communities. 'I was invited to meet up with Prince Charles to show him a few trick shots, and teach him the basics of the game. It was great – but even when I was with him, I was as drunk as a skunk.'

In spite of his drinking, Steve's career was still flying high, especially when he added to his list of titles the world record for clearances – clearing the pool table six times without missing one shot.

'One memory comes back very clearly now, although at the time it meant little to me. My mother developed cancer, and I hardly saw her. I went back to Bedford Hospital one day to see her, but was in such a rush to get off somewhere else that I didn't even bother to ask her how she really was. She'd had a breast removed, and went back home again. The last conversation I had with her really haunts me now. That Christmas in 1988, I was living with a girl called Lindsey, when Mum gave me a Christmas card. It was all about saying thank you, and the joys and memories of Christmas – and Mum had splashed out on the family that year much more than she normally did. On 10 January she rang me, and because she often rabbited on like mums do, I wasn't really listening to what she was saying. I just made half-hearted replies like, "Yeah, Mum, yeah, yeah, okay – I'll pass you over to Lindsey now – I'll speak to you later." That was the last time I ever actually spoke to my mum. Not much later we had a phone call to say she'd had a heart attack and had been rushed to hospital. She was in a coma when I got there. During the three days that followed while she was still in the coma, I managed to say to her, "Mum, if you can hear me, I'm so sorry for the way I've been. Please forgive me." For a moment nothing happened, then I watched as Mum actually opened her eyes for the first time since her attack. She moved her hand just slightly – and died. I'm so grateful that I was able to say that to her, because I would have had to live the rest of my life feeling awful and so guilty about the way I'd been towards her – and not just to her, but to the rest of my family too. My dad and my sister took their fair share of my dreadful behaviour. It made me realize that there are a lot of things in life you just take for granted, like their love for me. I just didn't appreciate it at the time. I would pay anything in the world to be able to have a five-minute chat with my mum now. But I can't. It's too late.'

For many people such an experience would be a turning point. Not for Steve. Living to excess had become a way of life for him. He was enjoying himself, adding drugs to the huge amount of booze he was downing. Before long it wasn't unusual for him to be drinking a bottle of Bacardi and ten pints each day.

Not surprisingly, his snooker form was beginning to suffer. As he turned up at exhibitions drunk, his world ranking started to go down. Just three months after his mum died, Lindsey met someone else – and she wasn't the only one to leave him. Other friends began to drift away too as he became more unbearable to be around. 'Of course, it wasn't anything to do with me, as far as I was concerned,' says Steve. 'I was blaming everybody and everything around me rather than myself for what had gone wrong. Then I went back on the Butlins circuit to Scotland, Minehead and Bognor Regis. I was drinking more than ever, not really caring about anything else, including whether or not I was playing well. I remember people looking at me sadly as they tried to tell me they could see my life falling apart – but all I wanted to do was drink and drink and drink. Slowly but surely, everything fell apart. I was losing money. I wasn't getting the shows I used to get, my career was going downhill.'

He was in a pretty sorry state when, in 1994, Steve met Linda. They eventually married on 11 April 1998. That marriage lasted a matter of days. 'Three weeks after we got married, I ended up in court because Linda wanted me out of the house, and I wouldn't go. I was drinking like crazy, and became really violent at the end. I never hit her or anything like that, but I was very abusive and frightening. Again, I thought it was everybody else's fault. I was okay – but because of everyone else my career was going downhill and I was getting in debt. It was important to me to have the XJS Jaguars, my house, the clothes and money, but I was spending much more than I had. One evening in June 2000, I was so low that I took my car to the top of Hengisbury Head, meaning to drive off. I'd just had enough. But I even failed at that. I didn't have the bottle to do it at the end of the day.

'By that time, I had lost everything. I was unshaven and looked like a tramp. I'll never forget being spotted by someone who thought they recognized me and said, "Oh, that looks like Steve Sanders, the snooker player..." They actually came up to me and asked if I was, and I just said, "No, you've got the wrong person." Then as I walked away, I heard another bloke say, "Don't be stupid, Steve Sanders wouldn't look like that."

'It was an awful time, a nightmare. I was homeless, and for about a month had nowhere to sleep except on the beach in Bournemouth. I'd just crash anywhere I could. For five weeks, I didn't bother eating because all I was interested in was drinking – and I could only do that when I managed to bum money off someone or other. Still it was everybody else's fault except mine. I felt sorry for myself, even when people said to me, "You need help." I just pushed them away. I didn't need them or their opinions.

'Then one day I was lying down on the beach, and I thought back to when my career first started, and I came down to play in Bournemouth. I'd stay at the High Cliff Hotel, I had a nice car, and everything was great. And there I was down on the beach, shivering because I had DTs. I looked up at the sign for the High Cliff, because you can see it from the beach – and I just started crying. Something must have come back from my Salvation Army roots, because I found myself crying to God that I just couldn't carry on. And from that moment on, things started to change. I managed to get into some accommodation that evening, even though I didn't have any money. The chap said I could pay him later when I got on my feet. I even went along to an Alcoholics Anonymous meeting. I was really nervous, but I went in anyway. I thought that they were all a load of idiots, so I walked out and went straight to the pub. But the following week, I went to another AA meeting, and then found myself going the week after that. I sat there listening to their stories, and eventually plucked up the courage to say what everybody says at AA, "My name's Steve, and I'm an alcoholic." I can't tell you what a relief it was to say it out loud, and all the people around me were congratulating me, telling me I'd made the biggest decision of my life. At the time, I thought, "Well, they all say that" – but I decided to take things, in the words of AA, one step at a time.

'Those AA meetings were held in a church hall, and one night in the church they were having a choir practice, but must have left a switch on, because it relayed the music next door to all of us. It only happened for a few seconds, but I heard them singing "Be Still for the Presence of the Lord" – and I just burst into tears. The others wanted to know what was up with me, but I knew they couldn't understand. All those years I'd thought I didn't need God in my life. I didn't need anybody – just snooker and booze. I had all the money I needed, women, you name it! But when I came out of the hall that night I realized that I was someone just for me. I didn't need fame and glamour any more. I could walk away from it all, and turn my life around.

'Mind you, that was easier said than done. My life was still in a mess, and it wasn't easy facing up to the real world without drink. I just dealt with it one day at a time. Then about five weeks later, I bumped into my wife, Linda. She had been so upset by my behaviour that she had run away to her daughter's house for five months, just to get away from me. She had the divorce papers with her, and I even signed them so that we would be divorced in July. But when we saw each other again, it was clear that I had stopped drinking. It was probably the first time she had ever seen me sober! I told her I'd gone to AA, and she was over the moon. We ended up going for a cup of tea – and we've been together ever since! In August that year we renewed our wedding vows. It was a happy, very emotional day.'

Nowadays, Steve is completely out of show business, and happy to be in the real world. 'I am working in my own business selling fish from a van to local farms, shops and households. Apart from fresh fish, I also sell frozen food and meats – and I'm doing okay. I've still got a few things to sort out – but I'm clearing the debts, and am quite settled. More than that, I feel so much better physically now. There was a time when my liver was so damaged that my count was 365, when it should have been about 40! Now I've stopped drinking, it has completely returned to normal. I've been given another chance . . .

'Now I realize that in life, it's the small things that count, caring for other people, being grateful just for every day. When I'm walking along and see a nice sunset, or when I think about my mum, those are the moments which are important to me now. Before I was just living in a false world, a cloud cuckoo land, as if I were in a pantomime for twenty-five years! I thought the high life would help me escape reality – but show business is not reality at all.

'Today I would say to anyone, "Be grateful for what you've got, especially your health and the love of people who stand by you" – especially for me my dad and sister, who I now know I love dearly. And always remember that however little others may have in material terms, they still have self-worth. Everybody is important. Everyone has something to offer.

'I've come through. I've lived long enough to make a fresh start. I'm lucky. I'm so grateful for this second chance. I may not have as much in material terms, but my life is rich in so many other ways. It's sometimes the things that are free in life that are the most valuable. In fact, most of all, I'm just thankful that I'm still alive . . .'

Jean

On the day the Second World War was declared, Jean Liddicoat and her playmate Roy ran down a hill near their homes in Kent yelling at the tops of their voices, 'When we get Hitler, we're going to roll him down this hill in a barrel!'

Jean was seven years old. It was 1939, and Hitler's troops had marched a relentless path across Europe. Next in line was Great Britain, and no one was in any doubt that Hitler planned to invade our shores. His military might had been proved as country after country had fallen into his grasp. His troops and landing barges were gathered in readiness. His planes outnumbered those of the RAF three to one. It was only a matter of time, so Hitler thought – and so did most of the families living in the South East counties, knowing that they were under the flight path from Germany to the capital city of London.

'I may have been young, but we all picked up the fear that Hitler was going to invade us,' says Jean. 'I remember my mum putting a little blue glass bottle on top of our dresser, and when I asked one of my sisters what it was, she told me it was Mum's poison. If Hitler came, she was going to poison us all. Every day after that when I came in, I would look up. If the bottle was still there, I knew we were still all right.

'Because I was the baby of the family, my mum and dad actually booked me on a boat to Canada so that I could be evacuated with relatives there, but at the last moment, she changed her mind, saying that if one of us dies, we should all die together. Just as well she made that decision, because the boat was bombed, and only two children survived from the hundreds on board.'

In early September 1940, Hitler began a determined air attack on London – but he hadn't reckoned on the 'Bulldog Spirit' of the British people, nor the organization, teamwork, skill and raw courage of the RAF. 'Our finest hour' – that's how Winston Churchill described the three months that followed, as Spitfires and Hurricanes took to the skies to face the might of the German onslaught. Time and time again, a handful of young RAF pilots were sent up to challenge the dark hordes of Messerschmitts and Heinkels, ducking and diving through the sky in dogfights to the death – often their own. This was the Battle of Britain when 'never in the field of human conflict has so much been owed by so many to so few'.

'We lived on the outskirts of Ashford where the fields are very flat across from the Romney Marshes,' recalls Jean, 'and most nights we would see hundreds of enemy planes going over to bomb London. At first, for us children at least, it was really exciting, a bit like a film we were watching in which the RAF pilots were our heroes. I'd be completely unafraid as I watched them overhead, the Messerschmitts with their white trails in the sky being chased by our lads in their Spitfires. How we cheered whenever an enemy plane was hit!

'Once I remember being out on the road with my friend Kenny, when a German plane flew really low over us. The pilot looked out of his cockpit and shook his fist, so we both stood there and shook our fists back at him! He didn't fire at us that time, but we were often strafed on our way to school. We always knew that we had to fall flat when we heard the sound of engines coming, and once a little girl and I fell to the ground as machine-gun fire pinged the gravel around us. Kenny really panicked and ran to the left to get over a fence into a garden, and when I looked up a couple of seconds later, I saw him hanging over the fence. I shouted at the top of my voice, "Kenny's been hit! Kenny's been hit", and his terrified mother came running round the corner. They lifted him off the fence – and he'd just fainted with fright!

'I shall never forget the day, though, when I realized with horrific clarity that this wasn't just a film adventure, but deadly serious. My mother and I were standing on top of our Anderson shelter cheering as we watched the dogfights overhead. Suddenly one of the Spitfires was hit by a Messerschmitt, and we held our breath as smoke poured out of it. Then we saw the pilot bail out, and Mum and I were cheering loudly – until we realized the 109 was heading back to shoot at him as he floated down towards us. The plane circled him a couple of times, and we could only look on as he was machine-gunned right in front of us. He landed quite near my house, and like any child I wanted to run over and have a look, but the air raid warden came and told my mum to keep me away. The warden went over to the hedge where he'd landed, then came back and said to my mother, "He's torn to ribbons." Although I was only eight, I listened to those words and they went right inside my head. They were words I've never forgotten. Suddenly I realized that it wasn't an exciting game any more. Before, it had all been just drama, but now it was personal. This young man who was looking after me was torn to ribbons. The pilots in those few little Spitfires and Hurricanes were our heroes. We owed them so much – and he was dead.

'I remember someone telling me later that there are always two teams in war, and that our side probably would have done exactly the same thing. That German needed to get rid not just of the plane, but the pilot too, because he would have come down, got up in another Spitfire and brought down other German planes. I understand all that with my head, but I've never been able to forget the horror of seeing him shot before me.

'After that, the war took on a dreadful reality. I'll always remember the day my mother thought our whole family had been wiped out. She'd heard bombs dropping, and ran frantically towards my school because she thought it had been hit. On the way, she met someone who told her the laundry where my sisters Joan and Joyce worked had also taken a bomb, and a little further on, she gathered that the railway where my father was a fireman had had many bombs dropped on it. As it happened, all of us were all right, but overnight, a white streak appeared in her light brown hair which stayed with her for the rest of her life.

'From then on, I was so afraid of the sound of the Messerschitt engine, and the sight of those planes has haunted me ever since. Even today I have a recurring nightmare of looking up to see them in droves above me, and have an awful feeling of dread. Here I am, 68 years old, and it still has its effect. If I hear a loud bang even now, I might fall flat. I know it sounds silly, but if a car backfires, I just want to hit the floor. And I often wondered why I always felt happier in very small spaces. I live in a tiny house with small cluttered rooms. I like being in lifts. I even went through a bad patch in my late thirties when I would go and sit in a large cupboard in my flat whenever things got too much for me. I realize now that it all goes back to our Anderson shelter, and the fact that I only felt safe during those war years when I was inside it. The dreadful fear of that time has never left me.'

Fifty years on, marriage and four grown-up children later, Jean and her husband, Denis, moved ten years ago into a tiny fifteenth-century house right opposite the gate of All Saints Parish Church in Staplehurst, Kent. Not long after they moved in, her eleven-year-old grandson, Philip, asked her if she was alive during the war, and in particular, whether she knew anything about the Battle of Britain, because he had to do a project on it as part of his History studies. 'So I sat down and told him all I could remember,' Jean says, 'the romantic stories, the gory ones too. Afterwards, he went into the church graveyard where he got into conversation with an elderly lady who had been a teacher in the next village. When he told her that his Nan had just been telling him about the Battle of Britain, she said, "Did you know that there's an airman buried in this churchyard somewhere, and that he was never identified, so no one knows who he is?" Philip spent an hour or so looking, then finally ran back home to tell me, "I've found it, Nan! The grave of the unknown airman! And do you know, a bramble hedge is growing all over it, and it's covered in long grass? After all those stories you've just been telling me, that airman is completely forgotten."

'Those words cut into me like a knife, especially when I went out with Philip, and stood at the side of the neglected, overgrown grave. The wording on the simple headstone read:

An Airman of the Second World War,
5th September, 1940
Known to God

'This young man had been one of my heroes. He died for me. And no one knew who he was. The mother who gave birth to him, raised him, watched proudly as he went off to war — she had never known how or where he fell, never been able to mourn by his grave, grieve as she should. And something happened to me in that moment — a relationship began between me and the young man lying at my feet. It was as if I was trying to repay all those pilots who had given their young lives for me then, so that I could live in peace today. I knew that by caring for his grave, I would be doing what his mother wanted – what all those mothers wanted who had watched their sons go off to fight, then never seen them again, never heard what happened to them. This was for her, for him, for all of them.

'So we stood there, this eleven-year-old boy and me, and we shook hands, solemnly making a pact that as long we both lived, we would always take care of that grave.'

In the years that followed, Jean and Philip kept that pact, pushing back the hedge, trimming the grass, planting seasonal flowers on the grave. Caring for that little plot of earth became very special to Jean, and gradually she found herself feeling more and more curious to know who he was. 'I remember looking down at the grave one day,' she says, 'thinking that I may not know who you are, but I do know that you were one of those heroes who looked after me. And I decided there and then that I would do my best to identify him.'

That search took eight long years. She began by asking local people in the village, especially the older members who shared their memories and stories. Then she decided to try and find some books about the Battle of Britain, but because they were very expensive, it took her some time to save up for them.

She discovered that the pilot's plane had not landed near Staplehurst at all, but some miles away at the village of Smardon. So why hadn't he been buried in the local church there? Finally, through reading one particular book, she found out that there had been an excavation of the plane crash site in 1970, which threw a great deal of light on her search. Apparently, the propeller, boss and front engine had been found, together with some coins and a box of matches, which proved the plane hadn't been set on fire. Most exciting of all was the discovery of a silver pocket watch which had stopped at just gone ten in the morning. The Ministry of Defence came up with the information that two pilots had gone missing that day. The plane of one, a Squadron Leader, had blown up over the Thames Estuary. It was known that the other pilot had crash-landed somewhere, but no one could be sure exactly where. The evidence from the plane site, especially that silver watch, provided the missing link, and at last, the 'unknown airman' was given a name.

Flight Lieutenant Freddie Rushmer was just thirty years old when he died. His comrades in 603 Squadron nicknamed him 'Rusty' because of his carrot-coloured hair. When he had joined two years earlier, 603 had been an Auxiliary Squadron, which meant that its members, like Freddie, were initially part-time. When war was declared, 603 Operations moved from their peace-time base in Scotland to Hornchurch in Essex. It was from there that Freddie Rushmer was lost in action.

Around that time, Jean was able to solve the mystery of how Freddie had come to be laid to rest in an unidentified grave in Staplehurst when his plane had gone down some miles away. She went to talk to the local undertaker, who by this time was in his eighties. He had taken over the business from his father who had told him how he'd had to go out one evening in September 1940 to pick up a pilot's body from a crash site. He remembered sadly that there wasn't much left to pick up, but he brought back what he could to his own church in Staplehurst. It was there that the vicar and undertaker buried him anonymously in All Saints graveyard.

One day when Jean was tending the grave, a lady came up to say that years before while her little girl was very young, she'd been putting some bluebells on the grave when three elderly ladies arrived saying that they thought it could be the grave of their brother. They had been very touched to see this youngster, Katie, placing wildflowers there, and they took a note of her address. The following Christmas, a card arrived for Katie from Agnes, one of the three sisters, thanking her once again. Excited to hear of such a break-through which could enable Jean to make contact with Freddie's family, she was thrilled to learn that although Katie had since grown up and married, she had always been a hoarder. Days later the good news came that not only had Katie kept the card, but that it had a name and address on the back.

That discovery was the start of friendship between Jean and Freddie's only remaining sister, Margaret. Sadly, although the other two sisters had hoped that this was indeed their baby brother's grave, found at last, formal identification from the MOD took so long that neither of them lived to see it. For Margaret, now in her nineties, that has been the source of great sadness.

She has poignant memories of their large farming family in Norfolk into which Freddie had been born last of all. He had been a 'mother's boy', quiet, good-looking, loved by all for his smile and striking red hair. Margaret recalls how naturally musical he was, loving a good sing-song which he might accompany on the banjo. Once he'd left home to work in the city of Norwich, he still used to come home every Sunday and for holidays, at first on his motorbike, then in a small car, to see his mother and father, going along with them to the small chapel near their home. When Freddie decided to change his job and go for a post as an engineer in Edinburgh, his parents had begged him not to go, but he got the job, moved to Scotland, and there joined 603 Squadron as an auxiliary pilot.

'The last time I saw Freddie,' says Margaret, 'it was in 1938 when there was no war, although we all thought there soon would be. I remember going to Yarmouth with Mother to buy material to black out our windows. Freddie always said that after the war, he wanted to go and visit his brothers who were living in Canada. But not long after that, I got a letter from my mum to tell me that he had been lost. Of course, we didn't know where he had come down, so assumed he had dropped into the sea. We were devastated. We were all so fond of him. I cried bitterly at the news. It turned out that shortly before he died, he had written to my sister, Agnes, saying that he had just lost a friend. Freddie must have been thinking then about the possibility that he would be killed too. He asked that if anything happened to him, please could we let his friends know. He was so young, facing the real prospect of losing his life, and yet he was incredibly brave. They all were.'

603 Squadron, which had been so courageous during the war years, was disbanded soon after. However, since then the Squadron has reclaimed its name and base in Scotland, and through them Jean has learned more of Freddie, his personality and the role that he and his fellow pilots played during the Battle of Britain. Gerald Stapleton is now more than eighty, but in the days when he flew alongside his commanding officer, Freddie, in their formation of three or four Spitfires, he was only twenty – ten years younger than the red-headed 'gentleman' he found Freddie to be. He remembers Freddie's quiet, winsome sense of humour, and the fact that when he told his team off, he did it with a smile. 'We shot down some planes while we were in Scotland,' Gerald recalls, 'but in the late August we went south to Kent to take part in the Battle of Britain. We lost a lot of pilots in the first ten days because we were new to battle. But we learned fast, and in time we felt as if we could fly a Spitfire blindfolded. We may have had butterflies on the ground, but real excitement in the air. When you got used to the aeroplane, you could do anything with it because your response was so automatic. You loved it, felt at home there, as if the plane were an old slipper, or a motorcar you'd had for years. I remember being in the air, seeing a formation of German aircraft coming over the coast, and all I cared about was getting into the best position to attack. Everything happened so fast, and we were constantly looking out for what might happen next. When I made a hit, I had no feelings about the

pilot, only the plane. It was all so impersonal. I've met a few German pilots since, and they say exactly the same thing.

'If you got shot down, you'd be flying again the next day. When you were up there and realized that you'd been hit, for a moment you felt sheer terror before sense took over. You had to decide what to do — whether to bail out, or whether you had enough control over the plane to land it. Many's the time that British pilots dropped in for cups of tea in corners of Kent after their planes had been shot down. People around there got used to us falling out of the sky!

'The first thing I knew of Freddie's loss was when he didn't land with me. We didn't know if he was dead, or perhaps a prisoner-of-war. But then you couldn't let yourself think too deeply about it. You couldn't allow yourself to think it might happen to you, or you'd never be able to get back in the plane again.

'I did wonder over the years though about what happened to Freddie, especially when we never heard anything more about him. I assumed that he must have been shot down over the sea because for so long I heard nothing about his body being found. It wasn't until Jean Liddicoat did her research that news reached me that his grave had been found.'

Finally, having made contact with 603 Squadron, and met not only Freddie's family but the few remaining comrades who worked with him, Jean felt that it was time he was given a proper service to dedicate the new headstone engraved properly with his own name. 'So I set about organizing it,' says Jean, 'determined that Freddie be honoured in the way I thought all those young "unknown" airmen should have been honoured. Through word of mouth, and with the help of a couple of newspaper articles, our little parish church and graveyard was packed by about six hundred people who came from far and wide. I shall never forget it, nor the most poignant moment of all when we stood around the grave as the priest made the dedication, and the Battle of Britain Memorial Flight swooped overhead — a Lancaster bomber, a Hurricane and a Spitfire. They flew over really low, just as they had more than sixty years ago. Our eyes filled with tears as we looked up to wave at them — Battle of Britain veterans, currently serving airmen from 603 Squadron, Freddie's family, friends and neighbours of all ages from around Kent. Shoulder to shoulder we stood, honouring Freddie, but in my heart, in all our hearts, honouring every one of those airmen who had died to save us. Freddie's sister, Margaret, asked that the wording on his grave should read, "He gave his today for our tomorrow." He did. They all did. That service was the culmination of all those years of remembering what I'd been through as a child. It had gone full circle. He had given his life for me. Now, as a much older woman, I could honour not just his life but his death too.

'One day years ago when I was tending his grave, a little local girl called Eleanor was helping me. As we were leaving, she suddenly said, "Nan, you're in love with Freddie." That quite shocked me at the time, but then I thought about it. Yes, I do love him. Love is the right word for my feelings about him. I have grown to love the man I now know he was. By taking care of his grave and discovering so much about him, I began to know this person, what he looked like from his photos, the type of man he was. I realize now that death is not the great divide it seems. I feel I have a relationship with Freddie, that we communicate across the years.

'And one day I'll meet him. I know I will. One day I'll meet and I'll thank that young hero who sacrificed his life so that I could live mine.'

Gerald Stapleton has visited the grave twice. On the last occasion, the eighty year old sat down alone beside the grave, and said to himself. 'So there you are, Rusty. We know where the hell you are now.' And there he stayed for a while, remembering what they'd been through, the futility of it all — and cried.

Swilly Billy

Billy Messruther has a lifetime etched in his face, brown and weathered from years of being at sea, fishing single-handed off the coast of Scarborough in his beloved specially designed boat, *Morning Star*.

As the seventh son of a fishing family, the sea is in his blood. The first Messruthers probably came over in Viking longships, and have been seamen and fishermen ever since. Billy went to sea when he was just sixteen, 'nowt but a bairn really' — and his passion for always being out come hell or high water, earned him the nickname of Swilly Billy. 'When there's bad weather,' he says in his soft Yorkshire accent, his eyes twinkling, 'and you're rolling about at sea, they call that "swilling". And because I seemed to do more rolling about than most, up and down the coast of Whitby, everybody just calls me Swilly. They used to say that I was putting in more time than the mollyhawks — that's the name in these parts for fulmers, a type of seagull which only comes inshore to breed! But they were right. For the last few years, I worked alone, so I didn't mind putting in long hours.

'I suppose it was because when we were kids, it was a real struggle. None of us had any money, and sometime we had nowt to eat – and as I grew up, I never had nowt either. So back in the mid-seventies when I came across a tatty old wooden ship, all run down, bit of a mess, I suddenly saw the chance to get my passport to live, a house for my family, all the things my kids needed. So I went to the bank manager to ask about a loan for six grand and told him I'd give it back in a year. He started laughing. He knew what state the boat was in, and how long it had been lying there. He plainly thought I was daft, but he gave me the money anyway. So I got to work. She was really tired, with an old engine, everything left to get run down and worn out. But I just didn't stop. I worked fifty hours at a stretch, day and night, then I would come in and get four hours sleep before getting up to put in another fifty. I was in a dream half the time, but all I did was work because there was no way I could allow it to fail. When I came in from sea, the engineers would say, "She'll never take what you're giving her because she hasn't been worked like that for a long time." So I told them that if she can't do it, she'll have to pack up.

'Anyway, I had her eight months before the engine couldn't take any more – so I had to go back to the bank manager. I'd borrowed six grand eight months before, and he told me that in just those few months I'd got the debt down to one hundred pounds. I said, "Right, I might want thirty thousand now!" "You can have anything you like!" was his reply. So I spent that money having her completely ripped out so that I could put in a new engine, and then just worked and worked and worked. I remember telling my crew that they'd have to ask a copper where their houses were when we got ashore because we were out so much. I'd come in about eight o'clock at night, land my fish, have a meal and about four hours' sleep, then I'd grab half a pound of bacca, and go off again for maybe two days. For fifteen months we didn't have one week without wages. It didn't matter what the weather was, we just went. I never slept on board the ship, so my bunk was always empty because I never let anybody take charge but me. A couple of times, I spiked the hatches on running home because I hung on until the weather was too bad to fish. That ship of mine was a first-class sea boat — like a duck, you could never sink her! In a gale, there was no other ship I would have been glad to climb on board from my own. Sometimes when the weather was bad, people would ask, "Who's out today?" And they'd say, "Only Swilly Billy." And somehow that nickname just stuck.'

By 1989, Billy had made the decision he would prefer to work alone, even though other fishermen thought he was mad. He didn't want to rely any longer on crew members who didn't match his effort, but shared his profit. So he worked for eighteen months with a builder friend and an architect to design a boat later called *Morning Star*, which was custom-built for him, with every control, window and piece of equipment perfectly suited to his individual needs. 'I didn't even have a cabin built on the ship because if there was only me aboard, and if I'm down in the cabin, who's in the wheelhouse keeping watch?'

Usually three men would be needed to pull the net in from the back of the boat. What Billy installed instead was a giant fishing reel which could pull four tons at a time. 'I could just pull a lever which would wind the catch in on hydraulics. They could do all the work, never get tired, never have belly ache, never complain. There's no messing about with them. They do as you tell them!'

Because Billy needed to go for fish that didn't take up a lot of room on the boat but still made a fair amount of money, he fished mainly for Dover soles, which would come close into the shore, and fetch a top price of three hundred pounds a basket. Sometimes, especially in the first half of the year, he'd go for months earning hardly anything. In the summer he might earn a month's wages in one day.

Swilly's enthusiasm for the sea has never diminished. 'It's

wonderful, the sea — no traffic, no cars — just wonderful. Of course, you'd be a fanatic, wouldn't you, if you didn't want to stop in bed rather than get up and go fishing in the middle of the night? But in the summer, it's daylight at three o'clock, and I've always jumped out of bed like a coiled spring. Within a second of being awake, my mind was on where I was going to fish that day, and where I wanted to be by what time. That was the challenge of it — not knowing what you'd have at the end of the week, except that whatever it was you'd have to go out and get it yourself. It was all down to you. And if Joe Bloggs next to me had caught ten stone, I would want eleven, just so that I could be top dog. And if I caught the same as a sixty footer with three blokes aboard, then all I'd get was, "It's all right for you, you have the lot!" And I'd say, "Yes, but I did all the work." But when that net's on the sea bed, the fish don't know if there are six fellas aboard with fourteen kids apiece — or just me. But it makes a difference to me. What's in the trawl is mine.

'Every now and then I'd pick up a really big sole, about two foot long, probably thirty-five or forty years old. And I'd think he's been forty years dodging gear, and now I've come along and picked him up. So when I got one of them grey old grandads or grannies, I would sometimes let it go, because we're all entitled to a break once in a while.'

By July 1991, Swilly had been fishing on his own in his specially designed boat for a couple of years. One day he was fishing about fifteen miles away from his home in Scarborough, near Flamborough Head and the Bempton Cliffs, which are very sheer. 'When you get to Bempton, you just look up three hundred feet of rock face, like the Cliffs of Dover. There's no way to get ashore, so I always used to think I wouldn't like to be wrecked there, because you'd literally run into the cliffs and that would be it. It's littered with wrecks.

'On that particular morning, my mind was in an awful state

because I'd been having serious problems with my wife. I was really upset, but I went out anyway. The thing about being on your own is that you've got to have a routine, and stick to it. It's when you break your routine that accidents happen. In spite of all the safety features we built into the ship, it's likely to be the simple things that cause accidents. So there I was trawling for Dover soles, doing about four knots, pulling my net around half a mile from the cliffs. It was about one o'clock in the afternoon on a fine day, with a long rolling swell, and I was going around a particular tow among patches of sand littered with wrecks and rocks, so I had to be careful or else I would bust my net.

'I needed to go down to the fish room, which is a compartment partitioned from the engine room, where the fish were kept, boxed and iced. It's quite a big area, sealed at the top by a heavy steel hatch in the deck, like a trap door. It lifted up with two hinges, and when it was open I would lay it back against the ship's side where I lashed it to stop it falling down.

'Now, I never went quietly down that ladder. I would jump down, maybe only touching a couple of rungs, and I'd be down. And the same when I came up – I don't think I would touch a rung below waist height. The underneath of the door had a rung on it, so when the hatch was open it became the top step. I would just grab hold of that rung, give a great heave and pull myself up and out. The trouble was that on that day, because I was in such a turmoil, I must have forgotten to put the lashing on. As I reached up with all my weight to grab that top rung, the hatch started to come down on me. It was a huge steel door, with combing that it fitted into on deck, a sharp thick steel lip. Just at that moment, the ship did a great big lurch, and there was absolutely nothing I could do. As the hatch come over, it hit me on the head with a tremendous clatter. But then as it knocked me down, my elbow was actually laid at a right angle over the iron lip. The lid smashed down on my elbow, splitting my forearm bone and knocking the knuckle off the outside of my elbow.

'I suppose I was lucky that it didn't pin me by my arm because then I would just have been hanging in mid-air from my elbow. As it was, I tumbled down about six foot into the pitch black fish room, and the big steel hatch clanged shut on deck, and that was it. I was locked in. I found myself laying on concrete, with my arm throbbing as if a hammer had smashed it. I could feel it was wet, so I knew that I was bleeding badly, and it felt broken because my arm and fingers just wouldn't work. So I only had one hand, and because the ladder was set back from the hatch combing so far, I knew it would be impossible for me to climb up with only one arm. Besides, what am I? Five foot five? It's six foot to the deck, so to lift that big heavy steel hatch at a right angle until it opened and shot back against the ship's side would be totally impossible from down below with only one hand. I had two or three goes, but with the ship rolling at the same time there was twice as much weight to shift, so it was just hopeless. It was a minute or two before I realized I was in serious trouble, and I just couldn't believe it. I had always been so quick and nippy, it never occurred to me that I could be trapped on my own boat.

'I knew the boat was towing at four knots, and that as she swung round before the swell, she would be going straight for Bempton Cliffs. I could tell from the motion of the ship that she'd straightened, and was no longer rolling across the sea. The swells were running straight to shore, so I knew that unless I could do something, I'd end up wrecked against the cliff face. The nets would be torn to pieces, the boat would just sink, and I would be totally and absolutely trapped. When I looked towards the engine room, the only possible escape was through a tiny little hatch where the propeller shaft was running through. The shaft is about five inches thick, with a great big foot-wide flange and huge bolt through it. I could see it as just a blur going round. I wondered if I could press myself up against the side and crawl through, but I knew that the flange bolts would chop me into mincemeat, especially with 180 horse power driving the engine.

'I just thought, I've had it. I'm going to die, because the ship would soon hit the rocks. And there was no chance of even the coastguards noticing I was in trouble and sending help. They were so used to seeing me in that area, they wouldn't think twice about it until it was too late.

'All I felt was anger. I was livid because I thought I'm going to be lost, and my wife's going to get the insurance money and all my cash. She'll be the poor little grieving widow for a week or two with everybody sympathizing with her and there was nothing I could do about it. I was shaking with rage — too full of anger to be in the least bit frightened. I would have kicked and bitten my way through the side of the boat if I could, but I was just totally trapped.

'Then suddenly, everything began to change. I was aware that the sound of the engine went quiet, as if I had water in my ears. Then I began to feel a warmth creeping over me. Even the concrete I was laying on felt warm, and yet I knew it was really cold and wet. Gradually I realized that the anger was flowing out of me, draining away — and I felt surrounded, overwhelmed by love. This horrible little fella, so full of hell — I just felt filled by love. It was wonderful. I wasn't alone. I knew there was a warm, comforting presence there with me. There was I, the biggest atheist out, and the Lord had chosen that second to come for me. It absolutely filled the ship. How did I know it was the Lord? Well, there are two forces in this earth, good and bad, and I've never heard of the Devil doing nowt good. I just knew all the anger was leaving me, and I felt so calm and quiet and good. It was an overwhelming feeling of being picked up and loved. I just knew with absolute certainty that the Lord was filling the ship, and me. Suddenly the fish room started to become light, and when I looked up I could see the side of the ship. The hatch was opening! It sounds stupid me saying this now. You'll think I must be losing my marbles, but all by itself, the hatch opened. I was in total and absolute shock. Even now I have a job to take in what happened, it was so impossible to believe. But I was up and out of the hatch and standing in blinking brilliant sunshine on the deck before I knew it. My mind was racing. I can't put into words what I was thinking. I knew enough to realize that we were still going straight for the rocks, but I managed to get into the wheelhouse, and stop her.

'I looked down at my arm which was completely covered in blood. I picked up the kettle which was still warm from when I'd made a cup of tea. I could see a hole sagging open showing the bone of my elbow. I just poured the hot water straight into the hole and swilled the blood out. Then I got a whole roll of kitchen paper, bandaged it up as best I could, and then with one hand got all the gear aboard. That was the measure of how well that boat was rigged. I put on the automatic pilot and headed for home, which I knew would take about an hour and a half. In the meantime, I got on the telephone to tell them I'd had an accident and busted my arm. I didn't tell them what else had happened to me. How could I?

'So the word got round — "Swilly Billy's had an accident!" When I arrived back, the pier was full of people who'd heard the news — even the dogs were barking it. There was plenty of help then, so I just chucked the fish ashore and got a taxi to hospital to get my arm sorted out. They X-rayed it, because my arm was actually bent outwards, and they sewed up my elbow where it was all split open. They said I had to go back in a week's time, but I've never been back to this day. And I know this sounds stupid, but in ten days, I did twenty press-ups on the kitchen floor. I took the stitches out myself, and was back at sea in two weeks. Just tell me, how do you explain things like that? Human beings don't heal up that fast.

'When I got home, my wife and kids were away on holiday for a week, so I was in the house on my own. I lived on pies and things I could eat with one hand. But I had that time to think everything through, and try and work out exactly what had happened. It was real shock – not the shock of the accident, because that didn't bother me – but the shock of what happened down in that fish room. I had absolutely no doubt at all that I was not alone down there. The Lord had been on that boat with me, and had saved my life. He filled me with love, and made me feel so totally different. I really haven't a clue why it happened to me. There was no sense or reason for it at all. I'd never prayed in my whole life. Even when I was desperate to get out of that hold, it never occurred to me to pray. Why would I? I was totally and absolutely anti-God, an atheist for fifty-one years. If I ever got the chance to give the clergy a bad time, I used to love it. I was really awful to them. If the vicar was on the pier blessing the boats and he came somewhere near me, I would really give him stick. The only time I'd ever been in church was under duress, when I got married.

'I think it all went back to when I was a bairn, just fourteen. There was a little lass who lived over the road from us. Her name was Joy, and she used to play with my sister. Well, she'd gone downstairs in the night for a candle, and set her nightie on fire. I remember seeing her run out into the street covered in flames, screaming and burning, and she was only a tot when she died. And I thought then, if there's a God, and he's responsible for this lot, then when I get close to him, I'm going to smack him right in the teeth! I looked at that little bairn screaming so awful, and thought, well, if he can do something about it, why doesn't he get on with it?

'I didn't know what to do about how I felt. There wasn't

anyone I knew that I could talk to. I thought perhaps I should read the Bible, but I hadn't a clue where to start. Strange things were happening inside me, so I was glad of that time on my own to chew it all over.

'Then at the end of the week, my wife came home with the kids. We'd been going through such a bad time, hardly speaking. But when she got back that day, I just loved her to death!

'You can't imagine what a surprise that was to me, because we'd been at loggerheads for ages. We'd been married a while by then, and had two bairns, a daughter, who was fifteen, and a son aged nine at the time. My wife had often gone to the Anglican church in the town, which was all right because Sunday was usually one of my best days at sea. I got a bit mad when she gave the church a couple of quid every week, because I thought, that's coming out of my cod end, that! But our problems really started while I was busy building the new boat, working all hours to pay for it all, and make ends meet for the family. Well, my wife had got herself all tied up with the Jehovah's Witnesses, because my own sister had taken her along there. They kept quiet about it for ages, because they knew how I'd feel, but when I did find out, I hit the roof! She wanted to take the kids along, and I was so furious about that. It was total war in our house, with the pair of us shouting at each other, and the family breaking up over it. My son wouldn't talk to me, or have nowt to do with me. It was out and out war. My daughter, Holly, just never shut up about wanting to go, and in the finish, what do you do with lasses? I didn't know what to do. With a lass of fifteen, I wouldn't know. That was her mother's department, so I let her go with her mother. But by then my son, who was only nine, wanted to go too. My answer was absolutely not! I wouldn't let him join that church, and that was that. It was heartbreaking for me, because until then he had been my best little pal. He just about lived aboard my ship, it was all he wanted to do. Sometimes he would be at sea with me all night. But all of a sudden, he was frantic to go to that church, and believed he would die if he didn't go. So at the time of my accident at sea, that was the situation at home – total war, with me against the other three.

'It was because I was so worried about what was happening to my family that in desperation, a few weeks before my accident, I had gone along to talk to the local minister. He had told me to pray. I said to him, "Pray? That sounds as much use as a chocolate poker to me! A complete waste of time!" That's why what happened to me on the boat had come as such a bolt out of the blue.

'Anyway, when my wife came back that Saturday, she looked at me and knew something had happened. Within a few minutes, she said, "Don't look at me like that, as if you're looking right through me!" Then she said to the kids, "There's a demon in your dad. Don't touch him!" She wasn't interested in hearing what had happened on board that boat – so even though I found myself feeling real love for her, it didn't make any difference to the atmosphere at home.

'So I was on my own. I decided that the only place where I might find some answers would be the church, and I felt an overwhelming urge to go there. So that Sunday I took myself along to the big Methodist church in the middle of Scarborough. I walked in, and a lady at the door grabbed me and shook my hand. Then I went up the stairs, and another lady came forward and shook my hand. Then a fella at the door gave me a book with a piece of paper in it. I went right to the back where there was nobody, in the middle as far away from everyone else as I could be. I was in a bit of a dream really. The next thing I knew, they were all getting up around me to sing, reading from the little bit of paper. I'll never forget that hymn: "O Lord my God, when I'm in awesome wonder consider all the words Thy hand has made." Those words just spoke to me. Tears were streaming down my face, although luckily nobody seemed to notice because I was so far away from everybody. It was just such a wonderful experience, thinking about the difference from the fella I had been three weeks before — I couldn't believe it. I really can't put into words how I felt. I was so different, just like that, but I'd done nothing to warrant it, or ask for it.

'I whipped out of the church as soon as the service finished, out the door like a shot before anybody could talk to me or nowt. I was even out of the door before the minister could get to the entrance to shake hands with the congregation as they left. But once I was outside, there was so much I could look back on and savour from that service. But I'd got the cart before the horse. I hadn't got a clue about the Bible. I had this wonderful faith, but not the faintest idea what to do about it. I'd always avoided talking to Christians, and had never heard of anything like this ever in my life. It was all totally out of the blue, like a fairy story really.

'I remembered one bit from the Bible that my daughter mentioned to me once, although I had no idea where to look for it. It was about Jesus saying that whosoever believed in him shall not perish, but have everlasting life. Well, those words felt like pearls to me. I supposed it meant that I could be part of this everlasting life, and not just die as I always thought I would. I used to say, "Just bury me in an old crab box when I'm gone. I won't be worried. I'll just be old meat then. You rot, and that's the finish." But suddenly this whole new world was opening up to me, and those words were the pearls of the job. I spent half the night searching through the Bible to find that bit my daughter had mentioned.

'I've thought so much since that day on the boat about why the Lord stepped in as He did. My tiny little brain can hardly understand it, but I truly think that you don't always have to ask the Lord for help. When he sees people in need, He must sometimes just decide to enter the situation. He certainly did with me. But I'll never be able to think of any reason why the Lord should pick up a mucky little rag like me and do all that, when I've always given Him such a hard time. It doesn't add up, does it?

'From then on, I was just different in so many ways. At home, for instance, I would have happily rung my wife like a chicken a few weeks beforehand but I found I just loved them all so much. I couldn't help myself. I still wouldn't let my son go to Kingdom Hall, but I was no longer angry, which confused everyone! My wife simply didn't know how to handle me. In the end, she said, "I want my old Bill back. I know what to do with him, but I can't handle the person you've become. You're a stranger to me."

'And the other skippers down on the pier thought I'd gone a bit peculiar too. They thought I'd taken a knock on the head from the ship's hatch and gone loopy. You have to bear in mind that I was a typical seaman myself. I swore like a trooper – never in front of women or kids, of course – but at sea the air was blue amongst skippers all the time. Well, after the accident, the wish to swear just left me. I didn't have to work at it. I simply didn't swear any more. And how could I tell them how different I felt? How could a fella like me, rough and ready, one of the lads, start talking about God filling me with love?

'Anyway, after the accident, I went back out to sea again for the first time, and was overcome by the feeling that the world was such a wonderful place. The sky was the bluest blue it could ever be – because suddenly I knew the Lord was there, beyond any shadow of a doubt, and He had made all this. Everything was so clearly a perfect jigsaw, and I couldn't believe that I'd never seen it before. It was August, early morning, with the sun just coming up. The sea was like glass. I could see God in all these things. Even though my own life was in tatters, I felt so good, lifted by it all. But to explain it to people? I couldn't really. I just kept quiet, chewed it all over, and tried to make bits of sense to it.

'Another odd thing happened. I was a real smoker. I'd have up to a thousand cigarettes a week. I'd smoked from the age of thirteen, and I knew it would kill me one day, but I still couldn't stop. I couldn't ever remember going ten minutes without a cigarette. Sometimes I'd even have a cig in each hand. I had the tobacconist mix me black tobacco, and I'd smoke so solidly, I've known my crew threaten to throw my cigs overboard to get me to come in because it was bad weather. But bad weather would never make me come in. Nothing would – except for cigarettes. Sometimes I'd gone to sea in a rush with a cig in my hand and one behind each ear, and I'd maybe got ten miles away before I realized I hadn't got my bacca, and I would turn straight round and come back. If I'd not got a cig, it totally ruled me. I would wake up at one o'clock in the morning, get out of bed and maybe not be able to find my bacca. I would just get in the car, go down to the pier, get aboard, find a cig, drive home, then get back to bed. I would be getting up for work at half past three in the morning, and the first thing I'd do was have a cigarette.

'Anyway, after my accident, I was steaming home one day when for the second time in my life, I was aware that the Lord was in the wheelhouse with me again. I recognized the feeling, as if someone was at sea with me, and they walked into the wheelhouse, and where they were filling the door, the engine noise went quiet because they blocked the sound off. In fact, I turned round to see who was at the door. I'd have been worried if there had been somebody there! But there was only me, yet everything had gone quiet. I could hardly see at all. It was broad daylight, quarter to four in the afternoon on a bright sunny day, but I could hardly see. It was as if I was looking through a frosted bathroom window. So I pulled the throttle back and stopped the ship, because there was a big tanker ahead of me. It felt just as though I was in a crowd in the wheelhouse, with many people watching me. That sounds funny, but that's how it felt. And for some reason that I'll never truly understand, I just gathered up all my tobacco, papers and all, and went outside. When I looked out on the water around me, it looked like blue glass, absolutely flat, not a ripple, and it was totally covered in seagulls, just sitting there looking at me. I'm sure now that they could see the Lord, because I'm sure animals are better at these things than we humans are, and I knew beyond any shadow of a doubt that the Lord was there with me. I knew the feel of Him on my skin from the other time. I just know what it feels like when He's touching you — a wonderful feeling, a warm glow. The gulls were sitting there absolutely sparkling brand new, like you'd just taken them out of the box, and the water was covered in them. And I had my bacca in my hand, and just threw it, the whole lot, overboard. Then I came back and sat in the wheelhouse. I sat there for about five minutes until it was just as though my ears had popped, like when you've had a bath. The noise of the engine came back loud again. I could hear the seagulls. And I realized I was on my own again. I put the ship in gear, steamed her forwards, and thought that the minute I get in, I'll go straight off and get some bacca. I couldn't believe what I'd done — not just thrown all my bacca overboard, but my lighter and all! Well, I got in, but found I didn't want a cig just then, so I unloaded my fish first, thinking about what had happened, then thought, I'll get some bacca when I go off. But coming off, I didn't want a ciggy straight away. And I didn't have a smoke on the way home, or when I had my dinner, or when I sat on the step afterwards having a cup of tea — all the times I'd usually have a ciggy in my hand. I just couldn't believe it! It was like a chain that thick had been lifted off me! I know a lot of people stop smoking, and it isn't such a big thing, but the big thing for me is that I've never wanted a cig from that day to this.'

Billy's experience on the boat was in 1991. Now, ten years later, he's only just beginning to make sense of what happened to him. 'I realize now that, without my faith, I would have killed my wife, and probably my sister too. I was already planning it. I'd even had a price for having her topped! The state I was in, so many things dreadful things were in my head, and I don't know what I would have done without the faith I was given. It was inevitable though, after my wife and children got tied up with the Witnesses, that our family would split up. Sadly, we're divorced now, and my son and daughter have nothing to do with me, no contact at all. I just hope and pray, though, that one day the Lord will find a way to bring them, especially my son, back again. I used to be so close to him, and now he's lost to me. It feels as though they all died. Once they joined that group, our family was destroyed.

'But if somebody said to me now, right, you can go back to before those days, and have your family, my happy, laughing, carefree lass of a wife as she used to be, my kids and me as I was – or lose them for ever and have this faith, there would be no decision. If hell froze over, I couldn't lose what I have now. I could never give it up. I sometimes feel quite a cheat, because I got this free, and I was such a mucky piece of work. If the Lord can pick me up, I don't think there is anybody past saving. All the awful things I did and said before, I can't do now, because I know the Lord's watching me. That's the change in me. I can never doubt His existence as many people do. In fact, I have a wry smile when I hear folk talking about whether there is a God. I just thank Him every day for the positive way He entered my angry and troubled life. The Lord seemed to grab me by the scruff of the neck and pull me in. He gave me the faith, when I knew nothing at all about it – a car without the handbook. I've had a lot of catching up to do. Now I have a big circle of friends from church, and my life is so enriched – and when it's over, I know for a fact that I'm going to the big house.

'One of the things I do now is sing in the Filey Fishermen's Choir. We go all over the country, visiting churches. And sometimes in between the hymns, I am one of the choir members who will stand up and introduce the next song, and perhaps give a testimony. And I'm sure now that part of why I was saved was to tell people what happened to me, how God picked me up even when I wasn't really worth the effort. There's so much bad news nowadays, isn't there, in the newspaper, on telly — but I can just see that people are glad to hear my little bit of good news. And I can talk about the Bible too now. I'm a bit thick, so things take a bit of driving in — but if God can turn round a mucky little rag like me, just think what He can do for everyone else!'

and get on with having another baby, and I was taken up and down like a yo-yo to specialists in Harley Street. Thankfully, I finally found a wonderful doctor who simply said that I needed to be left alone, that the others should back off and let me recover at my own pace. In my own good time, I could choose to have another baby – in no way a replacement for John, but another completely separate person. Before long, Diana came along, a dear and cherished daughter, followed by our son, Charles, who became Earl Spencer much later after his father died. But I'll never forget John. He was my child, and he still is. Sometimes I think I'm the only one who considers him as a person. John is still in my heart, and that's what matters.'

Johnnie and Frances were married for thirteen years before they divorced. She was then on her own for two years before she married Peter Shand Kydd with whom she shared twenty years. Much later, when it became known that Diana was facing turmoil in her marriage to the Prince of Wales, Frances's own life was scrutinized by the press. 'You'd think,' she says wryly, 'if you believe the papers, that I was all over the place. But there aren't so many women who can say they were faithful to just two men for thirty-five years. Maybe my record is not so bad after all.'

Frances's own experience perhaps made it easier for Diana to turn to her when she herself faced the prospect of divorce. Frances is immensely proud of all her children, but she admits to special concern for the daughter who grew up to marry a prince. They both knew it would mean that Diana would lead her life in a goldfish bowl into which the world peered. When asked at the time of Diana and Charles's wedding what she would most like to give her daughter as a present, Frances said that she would wish her 'privacy in her private time'. She never got it, and in the end, it was that intrusion into her privacy which hounded Diana to her death.

Frances was determined never to be the interfering mother-in-law, believing fervently that once her children had chosen their marriage partners, then they should work through their problems together. In fact, for nearly thirty years, she has chosen to live on a small island off the West Coast of Scotland where she has farmed, and run shops. If any of her children ever did ring up in a panic because of a crisis in their relationship, Frances simply wasn't able to drop everything to be with them, and that has worked out for the best. 'I just accept that no one can understand anyone else's relationship, and it's none of their business anyway. I'm here if they need me, but I don't go rushing in to give opinions. I think so often people try to be objective, but in the end they can only be subjective. Better to keep our thoughts to ourselves, and simply be a good listener.'

Diana was only thirty-six years old when she died on 31 August 1997. 'At two o'clock in the morning,' says Frances, 'I was woken by a phone call from a great friend of mine in Oban, who said that there had just been a flash on Sky News that Diana had been injured in a car crash in Paris in which her partner, Dodi, had been killed. I immediately thought that if they had stated that someone was dead, then it was probably a reality. So I said, "Don't come down, I'll try and find out on my own, and ring you if I change my mind." I had two telephone lines, but put the answerphone on immediately because I knew the press would be on to me straight away. They were, and my lines were jammed so that I couldn't get through to find out where she was, what her injuries were, or anything. I packed to go to Paris, although I didn't know where she was or what was happening. I just felt as any mother would that I needed to go to my wounded child. I was desperately trying to get through to my family, but because of the media trying to contact me, they couldn't get back to me.

'Eventually, I got through and was told that she was dead. It was an hour before the news was given out. I wasn't allowed to tell anyone or do anything for an hour, because it seemed that the heads of state had to be informed first. So I was in this amazing situation of being on my own as I was told my daughter was dead, but I wasn't allowed to tell anyone, or ask a friend for help. I thought that was totally unacceptable, and it made me very angry, but perhaps that was a good thing. What made me even angrier was a fax I received very shortly after that from a tabloid editor. It was a handwritten note saying, "I think I know more about your daughter and her injuries than you do, so please ring me because our readers would love to know how you feel." I thought that was untenable behaviour.

'The police arrived about three minutes before the press began to camp out on my doorstep, and they stayed until Wednesday when I flew to London. During that time, I felt happier, more in command in my own home. There was still such a lot to be decided, so much that was unknown – where she would be buried, where the funeral service would take place, all of that. It was a difficult time. My feelings after John's death seemed very close again. I remember hoping that God didn't want any more of my children. There was no anger. I vowed on that night that I would never be angry with anyone over Diana's death, and I never have been. Prayer has always been very natural to me, although that doesn't detract in any way from the value of other people's prayers for me. At times like that, friends carry you. Their prayers get you through. I do believe prayer is the greatest force on earth, and to know that you have the prayers of other people is enormously warming. I was very privileged to have that caring.

'But because of John, I know too that grief is a journey you do come through. Another time it might not be the same journey, nor take the same amount of time, but it is a journey. There are no short cuts through grief. You can't dictate. You simply face each task as you need to, be in control as you get through it, then break down afterwards. But you can't do much more than that. Sudden death is an enormous shock, and the only thing I could do was accept, because there isn't an answer to it, there isn't an answer at all. For all of us, there's a *time* to die, but not an *age*. Diana was only thirty-six. Sadly, it was her time. "Thy will be done on earth as it is in heaven." That's what the Lord's Prayer says.

'My thoughts turned to practicalities, especially where Diana should finally be laid to rest. She had become a Spencer once more, independent and herself again since her divorce, and although I thought she should be at Althorp, the Spencer home, I worried about her being buried at the local church. I couldn't bear the thought of people walking over her grave and gawping. I felt that the only place where she could really be at peace was on the island in Althorp's grounds, but I hesitated to suggest this to Charles because of the effect it would have on his home and family. As it happened, the very next morning, after I'd had another sleepless night, Charles rang to tell me that he had thought the island was the right place for her too. That was wonderful news.

'Looking back, even though I realize I was in deep shock, I am amazed at how clearly I was able to think and make plans which had to be settled immediately. Faxes from the family were winging their way across the country, and I am glad to say that we had enormous input into the form of the funeral service. In addition, we gave a lot of thought to who should be asked, who would stay where, who'd sit together, who'd do what.

'For me, the fact that the service was to be held at Westminster Abbey was a challenge in itself. The last time I had been there, I had walked up the aisle to marry her father. My fear was great. I remember going into the Abbey, and thinking when I got inside, "Well, that's one hurdle over." Then I saw a whole row of priests, and thought, "No way can I shake twelve hands, just no way!" Then a precentor invited me, in my own time, to walk to my seat. The girls, Sarah and Jane, said in unison, "Mum, you decide," and I said, "Now." So off we went. I remember thinking, "Show respect and dignity. Head up. Don't wear your heart on your sleeve, be in control. There are plenty of friends in there, and you can do this. Get on with it, do it! Lead your chicks. Forget the rest of the world. We are burying one of our own." By lifting up my head, I had a blessed piece of good fortune. I saw, through the screen which separates the nave and the choir, the Cross on the High Altar, and thought, "Walk towards it, fix your eyes on it, and don't look to right or left." And that was how I went up that long aisle, unaware of anybody around me, save the comforting presence of my immediate family with me.

'In the end, strange as it may seem, Diana's funeral was probably the proudest day of my life as a mother. I felt so proud of her, of my daughters who were rock steady in their readings, and of my son, who gave such a moving tribute of brotherly love, and expressed the thoughts of her family and the people who loved her.

'I suppose it was part of my conditioning all my life not to let go, to remain in control. I'd almost built a barrier around myself. I stayed at Althorp that night, then flew back to Scotland on Monday to find the press had come with me. For eleven days I was a prisoner in my own home because of the reporters. I set myself a target – I was not there for their camera lenses, nor to provide glib quotes, and that was that. I decided to give them nothing – and I won.

'Within three months of Diana's death, I had over one thousand requests for interviews, which was hardly sensitive. One American magazine wrote to me saying they were doing a tribute. "You will be interviewed," the letter said. It certainly wasn't a request. The first question was, "Who told you Diana had died, and how did you feel?" I did write back to them saying they'd won an Oscar for bad taste. I never heard from them again.

'Mostly thanks to wonderful friends, I got through those awful days – friends who would just do practical things like washing up, or making beds. Friends who would notice that there was nothing in the fridge, and just organize to fill it, or cook a meal. Friends who would simply leave an apple pie on the doorstep with no name on it. Real friends.

'There seems to be a perceived way of how things should be after a bereavement. And people so much want you to feel better. It is a very honest, genuine wish, but you just can't do it. There are remarkably few people who recognize that to stop a bereaved person crying is the last thing they should do. Honestly, if you feel comfortable enough to cry in the presence of someone else, then that's the greatest compliment there is. You can get on with grieving, empty your tanks. I often think we store up our feelings inside a sort of tank, which fills up and has a lid on it. If you don't let go – cry, swear, shout, scream – that lid becomes rather like a pressure cooker. You're so wound up and stressed. But if you can let go, perhaps through crying which seems the most natural way, then you can empty that tank. You feel an awful wimp doing it, but you sense your shoulders drop as you relax afterwards. Then perhaps you can have the first good night's sleep you've had in ages.

'I've never been tempted to succumb to either counselling or medication to help me through. It may be right for others, but for myself, I thought that if I gave in to doctors persistently trying to shower sleeping pills down my throat, I would dull my response to a challenge which would have to be confronted somehow. Anyway, if I wake up at three in the morning, it's not so bad. I get up and make a pot of tea, play some music, and change my mood. I get through.

'Sometimes people facing bereavement are enormously unkind to themselves. They expect to manage too much, feel that others are coping more quickly or more practically than they are able to themselves. And having gone through the loss of two children now,

I know so well how much courage it takes to face people again. After John died, I remember reaching a day when I felt strong enough to go into the local town of Kings Lynn. So I gathered up all I needed, and got going, knowing that I could abort the trip at any time and just scuttle home. I set out to see what I could manage, and then realized that people were crossing the street rather than speak to me! I felt like a leper. You realize that it's not that they don't care. They're simply embarrassed, and don't know what to say. Now I recognize that if you see someone who is recently bereaved, then providing you actually know them, you should go straight up to them and tell them how great it is to see them out, and that they're looking good. It doesn't matter that they're looking hellish. Just say, "It's great to see you, which way are you going, do you want me to come with you, and have you got time for a coffee?" Leave it to them, but make them welcome in the knowledge that it has taken them a great deal of courage to be out in public again. Say absolutely nothing at that point about their loss — only later on, if the situation and mood are right and they plainly want to talk. Be a good listener. Don't allow your own experience to dominate how you think they should feel. When John died, I remember that someone would come along who decided that because I'd lost a baby, what I needed was a holiday. The next one came along and said I didn't need a holiday, I needed another baby. It was the same after Diana died. "You need to go away, you need to stay at home, you need to eat, you need to go for a walk—" And all I really needed was the right company — someone who would do nothing but allow me talk, and be compassionate enough simply to listen. In such a tender situation, that is all that's needed.'

Diana's death touched people around the world in a very personal way. The result has been that literally thousands of people have written to Frances pouring out not just their sadness at the loss of Diana, but their own experience of grief. The effect for Frances has been a mixed blessing, sometimes comforting, sometimes an oppressive burden. 'Over the years since Diana died, I have done more consoling than being consoled. The number of people who come up to me and mention Diana's name, then burst into tears, is simply unbelievable. They're trying to be kind to me, but often it's really difficult to cope with their grief as well as my own. I recognize that Diana had this amazing way of communicating so that she was a very real part of their lives. It's thoughtful of people to write to me so caringly, but receiving that many letters is also a heavy emotional demand. I always feel very humbled that someone I've never met should trust me enough to open their heart to me in a letter. Often at the end of their writing, they will say that they are feeling better because they have poured out their feelings – and I am a rather unworthy recipient of that. But it does hold me back a bit on my own journey of recovery. I do love people, but I am also on my guard, quite raw and vulnerable myself, so sometimes I find other people's grief very hard to bear.

'And sometimes people challenge me in the most extraordinary way. One day I was at Heathrow waiting for my luggage to come off the carousel. Passengers are all hanging around there with nothing to do while they wait, so I was aware of being eyed up. I play a little game with myself, trying to predict who and what people are, and as I saw a little grey woman coming towards me, I thought, "I bet you're a nun, and you're Irish too!" She was – and she struck up the most unbelievable conversation with me. She said that she wanted me to know that she'd cried her eyes out when my daughter's coffin went round Hyde Park Corner. I said, "Oh, thank you." Then she demanded, "Why wasn't she buried with her father? Why was she buried all alone on that island?" Sometimes it's better to tell the truth, so I replied, "Well, in fact she couldn't be buried in the church because those at the church are all cremated, and Diana asked in her will to be buried." And the nun went on, "I think it's so sad that she's there all alone on that island." I wanted to say, "For heaven's sake, dear lady, haven't you ever heard of the Resurrection?"

The Catholic faith has become central to Frances's whole being. She had always been a practising member of the Church of England. However, when she first came to settle in Scotland, there was no exact equivalent of the Anglican church in her area. 'So I literally went walkabout,' she explains. 'I attended services of most of the similar denominations of Christianity, and eventually felt that I had come home when I sat in the Catholic Cathedral in Oban. It is a rather imposing building, but the congregation there have become my very good friends. That means a lot to me.'

In particular, one of the reasons she was drawn to the Roman Catholic faith was because she felt it allowed her to acknowledge the souls of her dead children. 'In the Catholic faith, you pray actively for the dead. You think about those people, and it's gentle and comforting. You know that they are free of pain and all their earthly anxieties. They're there, they're living, but they are just somewhere else. I think of it as a family which is geographically scattered. Some members of that family are living elsewhere, almost as if they were overseas. They aren't on earth any more but they are living. That's the promise of Christianity.

'I long for peace – and the one place where I always find that is at Mass. I find the Mass Service so directional. You're on a journey going somewhere, and you arrive where you should be during the worship of Mass. I go to Mass primarily to give myself. I know we are a united family there. I go for confession, thanksgiving, supplication, glory, wonder, awe – and I come out with purpose sustained. There's help and support for everyone there, and maybe challenge as well. The peace of the church is so uplifting, because the cross is there. A human being standing in front of the cross doesn't cast a shadow. Above the High Altar is the Cross, and no shadow can be there, ever. No-one can get between you and the Cross.'

It has been through her attendance at the Catholic Church that Frances has become involved in pilgrimages to Lourdes. It began when she had a conversation with a young priest in her diocese about pilgrimage there, and she said that she couldn't imagine herself joining a bus tour to visit the shrine, but could only think of going as a helper. Then quite soon after that, the priest told her that he had been asked to go, and bring someone with him. 'He said, "Come on, we'll go! It's real indian work, no chiefs." So I agreed, and went, and have now been about ten times in all.' For quite a while, Frances has been going twice a year, with the Handicapped Children's Pilgrimage Trust at Easter, and with adults from the Dunkeld diocese later in the year. 'The adults are nearly all stroke victims,' Frances says, 'some of whom live in hospital. Because of the effect of their stroke, often they are very hard to understand, and most of them are heavy to push in their wheelchairs. The children, on the other hand, are quite mobile, especially those with Down's Syndrome, who are particular favourites of mine. Sometimes we take other youngsters who are physically fit, but who have a difficult home life. At Easter, the Handicapped Children's Pilgrimage Trust more or less takes over the town of Lourdes — about five thousand children in all, having a joyful, noisy, wonderful time! While I'm there, I have a kind of tunnel vision, and feel very protective and possessive of my group, or the child I am looking after. They really do give us a great deal more than we give them.'

Over her years of living on the Isle of Seil, Frances has come to value her kind, thoughtful, down-to-earth neighbours. They are very protective of her, with an innate respect for privacy. This is a community which mostly makes its living from the sea, with many fishermen and their families among her fellow islanders. Tragedies at sea still happen, and partly because Frances lives with this community, and partly because of her patronage of the Royal National Mission for Deep Sea Fishermen, and the Mallaig and North West Fisherman's Association, she is often on hand when families are coping with the shock of losing loved ones at sea. It is among those groups that Frances has learned most about the need to be a good listener. 'I've done my fair share of listening with people I've never even met before, fishermen's families who've been bereaved. Sometimes I feel so inadequate, but they're warm, gentle people who have always given me a wonderful welcome. And I think that most of what I know, my experiences, have been what they've taught me. I recognize that they are able to heal themselves, with the help of a hug and a listener. In the face of tragedy, they grieve collectively at first, drawing strength from each other, until eventually they are able to become themselves again. Sometimes they compare their achievements to other people's. "So and so is regularly going to the supermarket, and does all her own shopping." And I just say, "Why should that make her better? What is she like at home? Anyway, I don't care about her at the moment, I only care about *you*." And I watch as their shoulders sag, because it allows them simply to be themselves, all they can be at that moment.'

Through nothing she has done herself, Frances has become one of the most recognized women in the world. Just when she thinks the attention focused on her is dying down, there's another book, another legal case, to face. 'But you do get more bomb-proof, less susceptible,' she says. 'I've learned how to deal with the media, to keep them at bay. I can be absolutely brutal if I have to be. People write from countries around the world, asking for two signed ten by eight photographs. For heaven's sake, people who *want* to be in the public eye have photographs. They probably have a secretary too. I have neither. What do they think I am?

'For years before Diana's death, and indeed since she died, I have had frequent requests from the media to share my treasured memories, but they remain zipped up in my heart and mind. I have felt I was being asked to give that part of my soul which simply cannot be given. It belongs to someone else.

'I do feel that all experiences, even if they are painful and unwanted, can be enriching. I think unless you have known profound sadness, you don't really know what profound happiness is. Perhaps you can't have real joy and contentment unless you've known deep sadness too. All I would say to those dealing with the pain of loss and bereavement is please, be kind to yourself. There will be times when your heart trips, sometimes involuntarily. Just let that happen, and accept. It does get better, become gentler, I promise you.

'I am the proudest mum and grandmother in the world. I'm proud of William and Harry and all my grandchildren, and of my children, Sarah, Jane and Charles. I'm proud of my whole family. Their example of courage and dignity will be remembered with all my love and admiration for the rest of my life.

'I know that grief has no agenda or timetable; that living is in tunnels, with occasional Rainbow Times. But I also know that, although the ache never goes, there will be gentler, kinder days — sometime. I know that my life will never be the same, but I do know that it will be good!

'On the day after Diana's funeral, when I awoke to another day of cloudless sunshine at my son's home, I found myself pondering how two ordinary people like Johnnie and me could have made that wee lassie, who went on to become such a vibrant and precious sparkle in the lives of so many people. My son told me there would be a boat on the lake for the rest of the morning. He asked if I would like to go to the island. At first, I thought not. But later, walking in his garden, I was drawn to the lakeside. The boat looked overwhelmingly tempting. I rowed myself across to the island.

'Returning I noticed that the thin covering of weed on the water which had parted as the boat passed through was gently joining up again, like a Final Curtain being drawn. A lone swan flew by. I knew that this was Rainbow Time for me. I felt certain that my beloved Diana was at peace, and that I was peaceful too. I felt that, though her earthly life had been short, her living had been complete and completed, and that all was well ... very well.'

Ruth

My friend Ruth Merry tells some of the sauciest jokes I've ever heard. Her terrific sense of humour can make her a real party animal, centre floor at a disco, downing a drink or two, having a giggly girls' talk about the male 'talent' around! Nowadays, she probably won't mention the world records she's held for swimming, nor the regional and national medals she's won for athletics, downhill slalom ski-ing, and horse and carriage driving. She'll talk about music, films, work, fashion and her holidays abroad — and the fact that she's been in a wheelchair all her life probably won't come into the conversation at all.

The list of Ruth's achievements simply makes your chin drop, but for someone who can barely move her legs, and whose feet don't work, she is just awe-inspiring. She was born thirty-one years ago with Arthrogryposis, a rare condition similar to polio which affects the joints, spinal cord, muscles and circulation. One in three million people are likely to be born with Arthrogryposis. 'And guess what?' says Ruth with a wry smile. 'I just had to be the one!'

It's not a hereditary condition, and there's appears to be no reason why it should happen to one person rather than another. When she was born, Ruth's body was as inflexible as a plank, and it was mainly through months of strenuous physiotherapy, which she was put through with great dedication by her mother, that Ruth is able to move at all today. She remembers little of that painful regime now, except that her grandmother told her she had to leave the house when it was going on, because Ruth's cries of anguish upset her too much. Ruth was a first-born child, and it must have broken her mother's heart to have had to inflict such inexplicable torture on her newborn baby. Now, although Ruth has some feeling from the waist down, she says her legs 'just sit there at the end of my body'. To compensate, her arms and shoulders are strong, although their action is limited, and her hands go back to front, moving the opposite way to most people's. But being Ruth, she's learned to adjust. If she wants to do something, she'll find a way.

What followed were years of treatment and operations. Instead of starting school like most youngsters at the age of five, Ruth spent that year in Great Ormond Street Hospital having major operations on her legs, feet and hips. That meant she started school not only looking physically unlike other youngsters, but was also one year older than them. Time out for hospital treatment accumulated, especially with a long stay at Great Ormond Street at the age of ten, so that by the time she left school after taking the exams most students take at sixteen, Ruth was eighteen. That age difference was a constant problem for her. She was the only disabled pupil in a mainstream school. Many children don't have the maturity or sensitivity to react kindly when someone looks different. Ruth was older and more mature than many of her school companions, yet often felt ostracized and patronized for being different from the rest.

Ruth was ten when she can first remember being acutely aware that her disability would cause her to be treated differently from others. Until that age, she had mostly been carried around by her parents, or transported in a blue and white buggy, but at ten, she moved on to the independence of a wheelchair. Her mum and dad took her to the local cinema, and were told by the manager there that Ruth could not go in because in her wheelchair, she was a fire hazard. The embarrassment of that refusal, and the tears she cried because of it, haunt her still. 'It really hurt,' she says, 'because all that manager saw was the wheelchair, and that's what I've had to deal with most of my life. Some people only see the disability, not the person. The same thing has happened to me several times since. If I'm away from my own home area, I might even now be refused access to cinemas because I'm a fire hazard. I just find myself making a joke of it these days, coming out with something like, "Do you think I'm going to burn the place down for you then? Burst into flames through spontaneous combustion?" It still hurts though. It always hurts.'

Because, as a youngster, Ruth always went to regular schools in spite of her disability, she never felt disabled. Then, as now, it was other people's attitudes to her which made her feel more disabled than she actually was. The reaction of some of the other pupils meant that she had few real friends, and got picked on a lot. 'It was pretty tough some times,' she says, 'although the bullying was more verbal than physical. They'd call me all sorts of names, and I'd be left out of things. I always remember one Friday afternoon during my first year of comprehensive school, when Mrs Sharp, the PE mistress, made my whole class stay behind because they had left me out of playing indoor hockey. It was wet outside, and we spent the afternoon indoors, but none of the girls wanted me on their team, so I was left sitting on the sidelines. Mrs Sharp said that I should stay and face them, but in fact, it was worse for me to be made an example of in that way. That caused even more problems for me, because after that I was called the teacher's pet. Of course, I was a year older than them so they already thought I must be a stupid kid who'd been kept down a year. I just became very quiet, kept myself to myself, and didn't tell anyone. After a while, though, Matron rang up Mum and Dad because I was going through a particularly bad period, and their worrying made it even worse for me. They kept asking if everything was OK, and I just said yes. I really didn't want to talk about it, or have other people interfere and try and fight my battles for me.

'I was interested in fashion and pop music, just like any other teenager. I remember Duran Duran were particular favourites of mine. And I liked going to films, but usually went with Mum and Dad, rather than anyone from school. I remember once a girl invited me along to her birthday party, and I was really pleased, until she said she'd only invited me because her mum told her she had to.'

It was Mrs Sharp and other members of the PE team at school who finally came up with a solution which changed Ruth's life. They introduced her to the British Sports Association for the Disabled. Through that, she came into contact with other disabled youngsters who had been going through similar experiences at school, but who were interested in sport, and determined to get to the top in what they were doing. Their attitude made Ruth all the more certain that she had to prove herself.

She started with swimming. Front crawl and breast-stroke had always been impossible for her because she couldn't use her legs, and her neck muscles weren't strong enough to hold her head up long enough to take a breath. 'I hadn't actually perfected the art of holding my breath for the whole two lengths,' she grins, 'and you're not allowed to use oxygen!' But she developed her own style of backstroke relying on the strength of her arms, which were very strong anyway because of constant use pushing her chair or transferring herself from one seat to another. Before long she was competing in the Eastern Regional Swimming Championships for the Disabled, and to her surprise and delight, came away with a couple of gold medals.

'I felt wonderful,' she says, 'when I was able to go along to my teachers and show them my medals, but then it all backfired on me a bit. The headmaster told everyone that "Ruth is an example we all should be following", and that made me more unpopular than ever with the other children. You'd think they would have thought, "Well, if SHE can do it, maybe I'll get somewhere too." But it wasn't like that. Just think about David Beckham today. He's really good at what he does, and yet he's always criticized, almost as if people don't want him to succeed. If you're good at something, and perhaps better than people who criticize you, then they want to drag you down.

'It didn't stop me though. From there, I went on to my first National Championship, when I was about fourteen. It was up in Darlington for a whole weekend, and I was really nervous. I did OK though, picked up a couple more medals, and after that I gradually built up until I was a regular member of the Eastern Region team. I represented them at the regional and national championships, and by the time I was sixteen, I was competing at the World Games for Disabled Youth.'

Those games were held over a period of two weeks up in Nottingham. With typical modesty, Ruth simply says, 'I competed in three sections – the 25, 50 and 100 metres Backstroke. I got three World Records. That time, from 1986 to 1988, was terrific for me. I was really on top form, and so proud that I had something I could show other people to say look, I may be in a wheelchair, but there's more to me than just the chair, and here I am proving it. I had represented the country in the World Games, and I came away feeling really elated.'

The natural progression for any athlete, having won the World Games, would be to go on to compete in the Olympics, or in Ruth's case, the Paralympics. However, the strict rules and regulations dictated that Ruth would have to compete in more than one style, and because of her disability, backstroke was the only option available to her. 'I was put in a classification,' she explains, 'for people who have more movement in their body than me, and a lot of them were actually getting out of the pool and walking away. I couldn't do that, which was so disheartening. Then again, I just had to accept it.'

As that door shut, Ruth began to diversify. She has always been keen on athletics, so decided to try her hand at competing in the 50 metre dash in a wheelchair, and the discus, which capitalized on the strength of her upper body. Once again, she got to national level, picking up a couple of regional titles on the way. Combined with her swimming, this meant a disciplined regime of training similar to that of any able-bodied athlete. She was careful with her diet, putting in as many hours of training as she could. And it was around that time she discovered another passion — ski-ing.

'I was sixteen when I first tried that,' she says. 'I competed in what is called the Summer League, on dry slopes. Mostly I was racing against disabled skiers, but eventually I was asked to compete against able-bodied. I shall never forget one time when I was racing at Hemel Hempstead against competitors from all over the region. I came bombing down the side of an able-bodied guy on the dual slalom, and beat him. He was pretty surprised!

'I used what we call a sit ski. It's a bit like a toboggan, except you've got skis. On the particular model I used, it had two skis, with poles attached so that you can push forward, left or right. My top speed would be around 50 m.p.h., so I was moving! Mostly I skied on dry slopes near home, but then we'd go off to Europe to train on snow, as a lot of British skiers do.

'I had a bad accident in 1993 in Austria. I was in a downhill race and lost control of the sit ski when it hit a patch of ice, which is something even top skiers do every now and then. I came really close to doing myself a lot of damage. I've still got the scar on my leg where I hit a rock, and I knocked myself out. I thought then that perhaps I needed to be a bit more careful. I might feel like Super Woman, but I'm learning that I'm not!'

I asked Ruth if she felt fear as she sat at the top of a hill, knowing she was going to hurtle down it at 50 m.p.h. 'Sometimes,' she admits, 'but I don't own up to it, not to other people. I've always been that sort of person. If I want to do it, I just do. I think it goes back to me wanting to prove that I might not be able to stand up all the time – well, I can't stand up at all or I'd just pitch over – but I really did want to prove that I could do the same as everybody else, and sometimes even better.'

Once again, the Olympic door was shut to Ruth. In order to compete, she would have to use a mono ski, which has one ski going underneath the bob, and separate outriggers. Because her hands go the opposite way to most other people's, she couldn't manage to hold the outriggers and support herself. 'I was so disappointed,' she says. 'I felt I was putting in all that effort, so why wasn't I allowed to at least have a try? I might not be able to walk, but I could go out there and give it my best. It's every athlete's dream, whether able-bodied or disabled, to go to the Olympics, and I was never allowed the chance.'

By this time, Ruth was in her twenties, and working for the Benefits Agency. When she'd left school at eighteen, most colleges were inaccessible to her because of her wheelchair, and it was suggested that she should go to a college for disabled students in Coventry. Ruth didn't fancy that. Eventually, she did an apprenticeship on a Youth Training Scheme, finally becoming a civil servant, using her computer skills to work her way up. In her present job, her disability is never an issue because she works mainly on the phone or in the background, but patience, understanding and a thick skin are qualities she often needs.

Ruth has had a couple of long-term boyfriends. The first she met through athletics, and they went out together for four years until she was twenty-one. He occasionally used a wheelchair himself as he suffered from slight cerebral palsy, but he could also walk. 'He was a few years older than me,' explains Ruth, 'but I felt a lot more mature and independent than him, so I knew it wasn't going to work. He was a bit set in his ways, and that wasn't really me at all. At some time in the future, though, I'd like to think I'll settle down to marriage and a family. Right now, I still want to do things on my own, but then many people are choosing to get married later in life nowadays, so I haven't written myself off yet! Often it's assumed that someone who's in a wheelchair doesn't have emotions and sexual feelings, or need intimate relationships with other people. In fact, some people don't even think we go out at night, so what hope is there? I remember one time when I had gone out with some friends to get a video at the local shop, and a woman pulled in front of us to park in the disabled bay. I said, "Excuse me, you're not disabled," and she replied, "'I'm sorry, I didn't think people like you went out at night." I just said, "Yes, we do, so will you please move your car?" I can be very good at staring people out. I embarrass my mum because I just sit there, or wheel myself round to the front of their car if they've parked in a disabled bay. One woman pretended she was reading the paper, and every so often she looked up to see if I was gone, but I was still there! She left in the end.

'Most of all, I just want to be treated the same way as everybody else. How would people react to me if I were standing up? I may be in a chair, but I am a human being, and have got a voice of my own. Sometimes they talk over my head as if I'm not there. Once I was flying out to America, and one of the staff at Heathrow actually asked the person behind me if I could get on the plane by myself, and I'd never met the woman in my life before! She said, "Why don't you ask her yourself?" and I said, "Yes, if you ask me, I can tell you what you need to know." I've learned to be tolerant, and just as people talk over my head, I have to let what they say go over my head too.

'If I need help, I'll ask for it. Sometimes it's like the blind man being taken across the road time and time again. I've had that. I live in Hemel Hempstead, and before it was all pedestrianized, I used to be escorted over the road first by one person and then the other. They'd say, "Let me help you!" and I'd try to say, "No, it's all right," but they'd take me over anyway!

'Sometimes people just see the wheelchair, and they talk to you as if you're really stupid, or they come up behind you and shout in your ear, "Are you all right, dear?" There are a few people on the swimming team who had a T-shirt printed up. It said, "Pat me on the head one more time, and I'll bite your *!*! hand off!"'

Ruth admits that she's not always easy to live with. Her physical limitations frustrate her, and the continuous ache in her joints, combined with cramp, muscle spasms and sharp pain, get her down. 'If my legs are giving me hell,' she says, 'and I don't sleep and get overtired, I do snap a bit. It's the people closest to me who bear the brunt of it. I know I can be really horrible sometimes.'

It's difficult to say whether her physical condition is deteriorating or changing in any way. She notices very little difference, and only sees her surgeon once a year at the absolute most. And perhaps surprisingly, she has no bitterness about being born disabled. 'If someone suddenly said that there's a cure for my condition, I'm not sure I'd want it, because in actual fact, despite everything, I get a lot more out of life than a lot of able-bodied people. I do more than most people I know. And I have such wonderful friends now. If I hadn't been who I am, I doubt I would have known them. My real friends have always been there for me. The ones you leave along the way maybe shouldn't have been called "friends" in the first place.'

Among the wide circle of friends she now has, for some years she kept in touch with Jayne Torvill, of Torvill and Dean. Because of Ruth's own interest in winter sports, she dropped them a note just after they'd had their own Olympic victory with 'Bolero', and had begun doing shows around the country. Jayne wrote back, and that was the start of a friendship which has lasted ever since. Perhaps more unexpected is the very close friendship Ruth has with the Hollywood actress, Linda Hamilton, known around the world for her roles in the television series, 'Beauty and the Beast', and with Arnold Schwarzenegger in *Terminator*. Some years ago, Ruth was introduced to Linda through a mutual friend. 'Linda had been told that it was okay, I wasn't a nut! Well, I was on my best behaviour – must have been on the tablets at the time! No, seriously, Linda and I just hit it off, and we've been real friends ever since. I met her in Los Angeles, and then she came over to England a few times so that we got to know each other better. I've also been over to California several times, and seen quite a lot of her. We've found we have a great deal in common. We've both had our knocks, but then we're both pretty determined. She's shown me not to give up. If you've got a problem, yes, you've got to deal with it, but with determination, you'll find your way through.'

One of the ways in which Ruth plainly 'finds her way through' is by keeping her sense of humour. Sometimes, when she has been embarrassed or hurt by the insensitive reaction of others, she'll use humour as a kind of defence. 'If I can see that people are thinking, "How can I talk to her, what should I say?" I start making jokes about being disabled – things like, "Where would you find a cripple with no legs? Where you left him." They either start laughing, or get even more embarrassed and don't talk to me at all!'

Ruth's interest in sport continues, although she's no longer after titles and medals. Nowadays, she's likely to be found thundering around a track in a horse and carriage. It's fast, ruthless, dangerous, and of course, Ruth loves it. Horse riding has always been a hobby of hers, since her early days at Riding for the Disabled. 'But,' she explains, 'I can't ride now in the way I rode in the past because my legs have stiffened up gradually, and it's uncomfortable for me to side astride a horse. When I was about twelve, I had a bad accident when I was jumping because I wasn't able to grip with my legs. I did it all by balance, and on that occasion the pony I was riding stopped at a fence, but I didn't. I went straight over his head, landed on my shoulders and broke my collar bone.' But then, 'knocking herself around a bit' is nothing new to Ruth. She's broken her nose playing rounders, torn ligaments at basketball, and seriously damaged her left leg doing seat drops on a trampoline when her leg got caught beneath her, and bent all the way back. Her injuries don't mend well, and her leg was swollen up for weeks.

With her big 3–0 birthday now behind her, Ruth is taking time to assess what she's achieved, and what might come next. 'I'd like to move on and do other things now. I've gone as far as I can with my sport. I've got a career I enjoy, but then, I'd like to do more. I've a great deal to thank my parents for, because they've brought me to the point where I would now like more independence. One of the things I'd love to do is to live in California. The climate suits me, and generally facilities there are so much easier for wheelchair users. In fact, I've just been accepted by a film school in London to train as an editor. I'm hoping that new skill will allow me to work in California. It might happen next year, or in ten years' time, but I've reached the point where I would enjoy a completely independent life. I've always set myself goals, and I know that if you really want something, you shouldn't give up on it.

'In a way, it's been tough, and sometimes I do wish I wasn't this way. I would be lying if I didn't wish that I could get up and walk, but I've been given the opportunity to get out there and show others that even if the odds are stacked against you, with determination, tolerance and a sense of humour, anything is possible.'

Tommy

We try to forgive without any regret,
But how could we ever begin to forget?

Tommy Cragie is in his mid-eighties now. He has eyes that shine with welcome, and a face lined with years of smiling. The walls of his home just outside Newcastle are filled with photos and momentoes of his beloved wife, Lily, their son Archie who died from meningitis aged only two, Lily and Tommy's twins, John and Christine and their children, the people he's known, the places he's visited. To meet him now, you simply see a proud, warm-hearted gentleman. But like so many of his age group, Tommy has a story to tell that younger generations can hardly begin to comprehend. It is a story of inhumanity, hardship, despair, resilience, courage and comradeship – a tale which encompasses the very best and the very worst of the human spirit.

Tommy was a grocer, only twenty-two years old, when he and his pal, Jimmy Walker, were called up to fight in the Second World War. Twenty local lads left Newcastle Central Station on the morning of 17 January 1940. They were hardly equipped for war, not trained soldiers at all, joining a group of Territorials drawn from the border areas of Northumberland to become a close community of Geordie lads. Theirs was a machine-gun battalion, in which Tommy was a range finder. First, they were sent to France to build an aerodrome near Arras, but when the Germans invaded Belgium they marched day and night back to Dunkirk, losing their commanding officer in a bloody skirmish with the Jerries on the way. The horror of war hit them hard, especially once they reached Dunkirk where oil wells were burning, bombs dropping, and people lying dead around them. With spectacular air battles going on over their heads, and plucking an RAF pilot out of the Channel as they crossed, the lads arrived in Dover to find another world. Everything was peaceful, as Red Cross women served up cups of tea and packets of cigarettes. They were home.

But not for long. All too soon, they were handed tropical kit, big hats and shorts, not knowing where they were to be sent. The Middle East perhaps? Their destination was shrouded in secrecy as they set off from Liverpool, across to Halifax, down the coast to Trinidad. They heard the news of the bombing of Pearl Harbor by the Japanese as they headed towards Cape Town, then up the coast to Mombasa, and Bombay. For them, though, the war seemed far away, as they cruised and entertained themselves around the beauty spots of the world. 'Jimmy could always do a bit of a turn on the stage, even though he wasn't much of a singer. He and I put on a little performance while we were on the ship. I had nice features then with a head of curly hair, and he used to dress me up as a woman! I put a couple of apples in here, and oh, the tales I could tell you! It was real good fun, because we were happy and free.' Their journey took three months, so that they finally arrived in Singapore on 5 February 1942. Ten days later, on 15 February, they were prisoners of the Japanese.

After surviving a Japanese air raid just outside Singapore, they reached the harbour to find that as they got off their ship, civilian women and children were loaded on so that they could be evacuated away from the area. A strip of water about three-quarters of a mile wide was all that separated the British troops on the island of Singapore from Johore on the Malayan mainland, where thousands of Japanese troops had gathered, waiting to invade Singapore. Tommy and his pals were told all kinds of things about their enemy, such as the suggestion that they wouldn't be too tough to overcome, because they were all peasants who couldn't even use rifles. However, as they swarmed across the narrow causeway towards the Allies, it soon became clear that the Japanese were formidable soldiers. Tommy explains, 'If an officer said, "Charge that machine gun!", they would charge without question, because they lived by a code known as "bushido". They would always obey orders given by a superior, and would rather die than face the shame of defeat or surrender. That's why when we were finally captured, even the most humble of Japanese soldier looked down on us. If they had been in our shoes, they would have fought to the death. But you know British people, we're not a belligerent country. My father was in the First World War, and he used to tell us some terrible things about war. I never thought it would happen to me...'

As the Japanese arrived by the boatful, thirty or so planes would come across every day to drop devastating bombs not just on the Allied troops, but on the two million Chinese people who lived on the island. They captured the reservoir, so there was no water to drink. Ammunition was low, and thousands of people were losing their lives hour by hour. By this time, Tommy was without his range finder because it had been blown up on the ship coming in, and as he and the lads faced what was obviously a losing battle in the cemetery at Bukitimeh Road, the main road through Singapore, word came through that fighting had to cease at four o'clock, because General Percival, the officer in charge on Singapore, had agreed that his troops could hold out no longer.

At four o'clock, the guns stopped, and a deathly silence fell over the island. Tommy and the boys watched as the Japanese came over to talk to their captain, before about two hundred members of the Northumberland Fusiliers were led down to a field at the bottom of the road. 'We didn't know what to think,' remembers Tommy. 'Some of the lads were very bitter, crying and that. We had no idea what lay ahead for us, we were entering the unknown. The Japs came among us, stripping us of our rifles, watches off our wrists, rings pulled off our fingers.'

The next day, they started marching, and as they filed eastwards for about fifteen miles, they were joined by thousands of other prisoners of war. They headed towards Changi, past the notorious prison which has been written about ever since by POWs who suffered badly within its walls. It was hot, about 90 degrees, and some men fared more poorly than others, especially those who had already been wounded during the fighting. Tommy marched all the way – and if once in a while they passed through a village where local people came out with a drop of water, the Japs would shove them back with their rifles. At Changi, they were given barbed wire and told to build a fence around themselves. Once a perimeter fence had been erected, each battalion was allocated its own corner – and there they sat for about three months. And then in June 1942, six hundred of the men were told they were going to Thailand, where things were a lot easier and they might get better treatment. Two bowls of rice a day were hardly enough to keep grown men fit and healthy. They were hungry, and the news of their move seemed hopeful. They were going to build a railway. What they couldn't know then was that this line would later become notorious around the world as 'The Death Railway'.

'The Japs wanted to capture Burma, remember,' explains Tommy. 'They were plundering oil and all kinds of other valuable goods from Singapore and beyond, but if they took their ships round the coast of Burma and Singapore, they were going to find themselves facing British submarines. They'd tried it, and got a few ships sunk – so they thought of the idea of building a railway across virgin jungle. It had been tried before, but it had proved just too horrendous. Anyway, now they had all this cheap labour – not just us, but loads of Chinese, Tamils, Malayans – there was a right mix of people. They moved us up to Nong Pladuck where we started piling up rails, sleepers, everything that was needed for the railway. Then we moved further up. Jimmy Walker and his gang had been sent up earlier than us, and were working further up the line building the embankment to lay the lines on. Then they came down to join us at Nong Pladuck.

'Our commanding officer was a Major Flowers, and he was a great fella. The Japs respected him because he was about six foot three, and wore a big topi, a hat like a copper's helmet. If the Japs pushed you around, he would speak up for you. And there were times when we certainly needed that. Mind you, at that time they weren't that cruel, not at the start. But when we got really working on the line, word came through that they had to speed the job up. All the time they used to shout, "Speedo! Speedo!" – and if they didn't think you were working hard enough, you'd get a bamboo stick across your back. The way we worked was that two men had to collect a sleeper from a truck, then carry it between them and lay it on the track. Then the rail gang would arrive to put the lines down. You know, it was all co-ordinated. Put the tracks down, then other lads came behind and fixed the rail to the sleepers with big spikes. The rail was joined together by fish plates with bolts which were fixed to the sleepers. Sometimes as we were hammering in the spikes, they used to jump out and get our legs, because we were all barefooted – no shoes or nowt. We only had a loin cloth around here. I've often said that convicts were like film stars compared to us because we were a really rough lot. But when those spikes dug into you, flies got into the wound, and gangrene would set in. There was a fella there at a big hospital camp called Chung Kai, an Australian surgeon known as Weary Dunlop, who used to amputate legs every day. Mind, they made some marvellous legs out of bamboo.

'And, of course, the Japs were always screaming for more work. Sometimes we'd struggle on nearly all day in temperatures of around 120 degrees. Not only hot, but when the monsoons came, you were up to your knees in water trying to work in those conditions. It was really terrible. But I took it all in my stride. The only thing I had was malaria – but then cholera broke out. If you drank any water without getting it boiled, that was fatal as the river was so dirty. There were dead cattle floating in it – dead bodies too, sometimes. The cooks from the cook house used to draw water from the river, and boil it.

'We used to get up as soon as the sun shone. First thing in the morning, they would bring us a big hot water canister with a few tea leaves thrown into it. It didn't really taste anything like tea, but it was a thirst quencher.

'Slowly, really slowly, we advanced. It was horrendous because a lot of streams used to run down to the big river – the River Kwai. That had to be bridged. They had lads up in the jungle chopping down trees, some of them bold enough to ride elephants to pull the biggest trees down. That was hard. I was never on that job, but I used to see them. They'd pull a big rope up with a metal contraption on the end, and that used to bring the trees on to the surface of the river. There was no concrete, or anything like that. It was just a haphazard affair to bridge the streams. Once they got the big trees in, they were joined up to each other.

'As we moved up the line, we would go into the jungle to chop down huge bamboo to make a frame over which we'd throw tarpaulin so that we could sleep under it. We had to make a little platform about eighteen inches off the ground, because it was quite damp, especially when it rained so much — and of course, there were snakes! There was a snake in my bed one night when I got back. Well, you couldn't call it a bed because they were just bamboo slats made from opening up one side of the thick round bamboo stem until it made a flat surface. We just had rice sacks for bed clothes. We'd put two down on the bamboo because it was hard, you know, and then because it got cold at night, we used to sleep under other sacks. There were loads of them knocking about. Of course, some of the lads couldn't stand the sun, and their skin would come up in big scabs, so they used to wear rice sacks on their bodies. They'd tear a hole in the bottom, and two holes at the side, and put it over their shoulders.

'We would work about fifteen hours a day, and then little trucks would run us back either down the road or the railway to our tents. Our meal after work was always rice and stew. Sometimes you'd get a bit of fish in it. Mind, they had a good way of catching fish, the Japs. I was known as a canny swimmer, so I would often be among five or six Fusiliers they'd pick when they were going for fish for the cook house. They'd take us down to a quiet bay on the river, then throw in three or four hand grenades. Boom! Hundreds of fish floated to the top, then I had to go out with a basket and collect them.

'There was so much wildlife in the jungle. I remember one day when millions of little white butterflies were blown up the line by the wind, and we were all covered in them. I'll never forget that. And there were other butterflies there as big as your hand, and some really beautiful birds.

'By this time, cholera was really taking grip. It wasn't contagious, thank God, but some of the fellas started drinking water that hadn't been boiled, and they got it. They had diarrhoea, and were passing blood all day — cholera is such a terrible illness. Of course, they went right skinny — and if you couldn't work, you were no good to the Japanese. In fact, if you didn't work, you got nothing, so your friends had to help you. We used to get ten cents a day, which was worth a few coppers. From that ten cents everyone used to chip in a couple to provide money for the sick lads because we knew the Japanese would rather see them dead than get better.

'The Japs seemed obsessed with getting the railway finished faster and faster, and they used to lash some of the lads terrible. Of course, the worst thing you could ever do to a Japanese was to retaliate. They used to love picking on the big fellas, especially the big Australians. The little Japs would delight in picking on them — and if they ever tried to fight back, ward them off, perhaps give them a punch, then they'd be jumped on and beaten by about six Japanese until they were barely alive. It was awful.

'While we were building the railway, four of our lads tried to escape, but were captured. They brought them back, made them dig their own graves, then shot them dead. One of them was our sergeant, Sergeant Ray. He was a nice man, a regular soldier. It was so sad. But it made sure that none of the rest of us tried to escape. Anyway, where could we go?

'Do you know, I never thought that I would die there. I've always been a Methodist, you see, and had a strong faith. I knew we'd get free some day. God's on the side of the right, so I knew we would win the war. I never lost hope.

'We had no idea, though, what was going on in the war. We were just cut off from the world really. But you picked up little bit of information here and there — maybe a Jap would have a newspaper with a map on it, and when he threw it down, we would pick it up. We knew the Americans were advancing into the Philippines, so we did get the odd piece of heartening news.

'Eventually we had laid about 180 miles of track, and met up at Nikki with another gang with a few Americans in it who had been working their way down from Burma. Our next job was chopping down trees with great big saws, then cutting the trunks into sections with axes. Then we'd pile the pieces up along the line so that it could be used as fuel by trains which by that time were running back and forward along the line.

'We finished the line in October 1943, 200 odd kilometres of it. Then it was decided that the fittest of us should be sent back down the line to Nong Pladuck, so that we could be shipped to Japan. Jimmy and I didn't know how we felt to be among the lads chosen to go. What could we do? We didn't have a choice.

'So we were sent back down to Singapore and boarded a cargo ship where we were ordered down into the hold. It was only three foot high, and more than three hundred of us were crammed in there. All we could do was crawl in and sit with our knees up because we certainly couldn't stand up inside. In fact, the Japanese sailors weren't too bad. We were on that ship for twenty-four days, and every now and then they'd get us all up on deck and turn the hosepipe on us. It cooled us down a treat.

'We were travelling in a convoy of ships all full of prisoners, and when we got to Formosa (which is called Taiwan now), American submarines attacked us, and sank about six ships. Thousands of prisoners were drowned on that trip, and the Americans only managed to pick up seventy or so of them from the sea. But thank God, our ship was lucky because we just sailed through unscathed. We landed at the very bottom of Japan, and one of the worst experiences I can remember was when we were marched off the ship to the train. The Japanese in that big town of Mogi were lined up on the roadside, spitting at us and calling us names — because, let's face it, we were a really scruffy, unhealthy lot. We were thin, and could only shave if we managed to get hold of a knife which would hardly do the job at all. No wonder the Japs gave us such a hard time.

'Anyway, we got on a train, then the blinds were drawn so that we couldn't see where we were going. We travelled for two days before we came to a place that we later learned was called Iruka. That's a name I'll never forget – in fact, all the lads who were sent to that place have been known as the Iruka Boys ever since. We found ourselves right up in the mountains in an absolutely beautiful area where there was a big copper mine. We were taken to a camp which seemed like luxury to us after Thailand. They even issued us with a pair of rubber boots each, which was great because we'd been in bare feet all the time in the jungle. The only trouble was that Japanese boots are different to ours, because they had a separate place for the big toe. And even though the Japs had tiny feet, they had obviously got a job lot of Size Nines for us. I only took a seven in those days, so my feet used to flop all over the place!

'Around the camp was a fence to keep us separate from the village of Iruka. We'd never needed fences in the jungle because there was nowhere to go, so being fenced in felt quite strange. But we did have reasonable barracks, with a straw mat each and a couple of blankets, along with a bowl for rice, a cup and a spoon. And we were given three meals of rice a day. In the morning, it was sloppy stuff called pap rice, where lots of water was added to make it look more than it was. Then there was a cup of what they called "liquid" – even they couldn't call it tea! We got a bit of fish, and even meat, now and again.

'Our job was to drill copper out of the mine. We went into the mountain tunnel, then drilled into the ceiling, or wherever a vein of copper had been spotted. We had to drill a hole up into the vein, then the Japs came along and put dynamite in to blow the ore out. Then we'd put the ore into tubs and pushed them out. We were allocated so much work a day – say two men would fill five tubs with ore from a big heap. We wore our pants and green tops made from dyed rice sacks – and because they weren't interested in our names, we each had a number stamped on the back. I was No. 59. And so that we could see in the mine, we had carbide lamps. When water is put on to carbide it makes a gas which you can light. If we ran out of water, we had to have a wee to make the lamps work!

'One day, I was working with a big Scotsman called Jock, and we were both feeling off colour, so we fell asleep. That night, our numbers were called out – Jock and me who hadn't been working hard enough, and two other lads, one of whom had been "spreading propaganda" around the mine saying that when he got free, he was going to do the Japs in. The Japanese officer facing us that night had glasses with very thick lenses, and he was really evil. He carried a stick the size of a sword, and he would just swing it with all his might and wallop you right across the head. Well, he hit Jock first, and he went down in a heap. Then he hit me hard over my right ear – and from that moment, I've been stone deaf in that ear. In the end, all four of us were lying there, and he started kicking us mercilessly. That officer was a brute – he got seven years for war crimes after the war, so I heard. Then we were thrown into the prison hut with nothing to eat. It was really harsh.'

Tommy, Jimmy and their good friend, Joe Cummings, arrived in that camp in June 1944, and it was in August the following year that the war ended. News had been filtering through to the men that the Americans were on their way. They'd seen American bombers overhead, and the Japs were obviously becoming very tense. They didn't know about the atom bombs on Hiroshima and Nagasaki, but they realized that something dreadful had happened because the Japs were really terrified, running down the mine every time the air raid siren sounded in the village. 'It's just as well for us,' Tommy says, 'that those atom bombs were dropped, because we now know that some of our lads were detailed off to dig all day in the hillside making a huge cavern. If the Americans invaded Japan, the plan was that all prisoners like us should be taken into those places and shot, rather than allow us the chance to help the Allied effort.

'On August 15, everything stopped and went quiet. We wondered why there was no air raid siren that day. Then we realized that the Japanese soldiers had left. What followed then were twenty-four wonderful days for all of us. There was plenty of rice in the stores, and some of the lads even went out in the fields and shot a big bullock, so we had some great meat soups! During that time, an aircraft dropped leaflets on our camp saying they were on their way, and that they were going to drop food for us.

'About three hundred men were left in the camp, but sixteen had died during the time we were there. Some of them arrived with malaria, and just weren't strong enough to make it. Two or three were killed in the mine, falling down the shaft. One of my best pals, Albert Williamson, a Fusilier from Berwick, he died there – and he was such a nice lad. So what we did before we left the camp for good was to build a wooden cross on which someone carved all the names of the lads who had died there – the ones who never managed to make it home. It was a very basic structure, the best we could manage, but that memorial meant a lot to all of us.

'Then the great day arrived. On 9 September 1945, a convoy of American trucks arrived to take us down to the seashore about twenty miles away. The local kids were lining the streets waving flags and shouting "sayonara". You have to remember that the ordinary Japanese people were as fed up with the war and the military as we were. They weren't getting fed either. They were poor and hungry, and the soldiers would take whatever they needed to look after themselves first. Those poor people, they were as pleased as we were that the war was over.

'I'll never forget looking out to sea where on the horizon American liberty boats were waiting to take us out of Japan. Freedom at last. I weighed six and a half stone, just existing really.

Until that moment, the only way to get free would have been dying. Some of the lads just gave up and preferred to die. When your body is wracked with illness and hunger, and there's no medicine, what have you got to live for? I left Japan full of relief to be alive and going home at long, long last. We had been through such a lot, seen inhuman sights that I'll never forget as long as I live.

'How could we ever forgive cruelty like that?'

More than forty years later, towards the end of the eighties, an article appeared in a Roman Catholic magazine called 'Far East'. It was written by Father Cyril Murphy describing somewhere he had recently come across which he described as 'a place in Japan which is forever England'. He had found a beautiful cross and marbled memorial engraved with the names of sixteen British soldiers who had died as prisoners of war in a mountainous region some 350 miles south-west of Tokyo. What surprised and moved him was the bunch of fresh flowers placed at the memorial. Enquiring locally, he discovered that the senior citizens of the local village, called Itaya, had volunteered to take responsibility for caring for it. The article finished with the priest wondering if a village could be found in any other part of the world where people displayed such a generous outlook towards a former enemy.

Back in Newcastle, it was Joe Cummings who first came across the article. When he read about the camp where 300 Fusiliers had been set to work during the war years, his response was typical. 'Ee, that's our camp, man!' He immediately wrote a letter to Father Cyril, which was passed on to the people of the village of Iruka, although its name had been changed over the years to Itaya. One elderly lady in the village had spoken often to her daughter, Keiko, about the British soldiers based there during the war, how they'd all been such gentlemen, and how, before they left, they had erected a simple wooden cross in honour of their colleagues who had died there. That cross had disintegrated with time, but the memory of the thin, hardworking POWs had stayed with the older generation of villagers, so that eventually they decided to replace the original cross with a new one, and a fine marble memorial stone lovingly engraved with the names of the sixteen soldiers who had never managed to reach the shores of England again. For years, the villagers had tended the memorial, decorating it with fresh flowers. Keiko had grown up to move to London where she was married to an Englishman when her mother sent her a copy of Joe's letter. It had been her fervent wish for some time to contact the relatives of the dead soldiers, and to meet as many of the former POWs as possible. The 'Far East' article and Joe's letter provided the link she needed.

The outcome of her involvement was that in October 1992, twenty-eight of the Iruka Boys, led by their former chaplain, arrived in Japan on a 'Pilgrimage of Reconciliation'. The people of the village were so anxious the Boys should accept the invitation that they organized a nationwide appeal for funds, collecting six and a half million yen towards the cost of the trip. At the start of 1944, they had stepped off the train in rags, filthy dirty, emaciated and exhausted, to be treated with derision. In 1992, they arrived as VIPs, met by a band, local dignitaries, television cameras, and streets lined with people waiting to greet and welcome them. A banquet and a village sports day were organized in their honour. Everyone seemed to be there, including some men who during the war had been high school students forced by the military to work in the mine alongside the prisoners. One of them, Nakahara, called out Jimmy's name the moment he saw him. He had been about sixteen when he'd worked with Jimmy crushing iron ore – and after all those years, he had never forgotten him, or his name!

It was an emotional trip they made back to the mine in which they had spent so many back-breaking hours. 'I recognized it straight away,' says Tommy, 'with the mountains all around it. I remembered how we used to march up to the entrance at the crack of dawn every morning, where we'd have to bow to the guard on duty, and be counted in and out. That entrance was still there, although the shafts had long been closed. I'd never really noticed before what beautiful countryside it was – in fact, these days it's a place where people go for their holidays!'

But the highlight for the visit without doubt was the large gathering for the service of prayers and wreath-laying held at the memorial. 'We shed tears,' says Tommy. 'I did anyway. We all cried. We couldn't help it, especially when each of us laid a white chrysanthemum, the national flower of Japan, in front of the cross. Joe said later that as he watched some of the older members of the local community also laying chrysanths, he wondered what their thoughts were. We were so proud of what they had done in creating this beautiful memorial to our comrades. Let us pray that in future years, never again will we send our offspring to war. It achieves nothing.'

For Jimmy too, it was a very emotion-charged visit. He had left at the end of the war full of hatred and bitterness towards all Japanese people, but the prayer service and the kindness of the villagers he met during this return trip had opened his eyes to see the goodness of the ordinary Japanese people, many of whom had also suffered under the military control of the war years. 'I can never forgive,' he said, 'only God can do that – but it has taken away the cancer of hatred which festered away inside me all these years.'

After the war, Tommy, Jimmy, Joe and other surviving Iruka Boys had come back to the Newcastle area, old beyond their young years, to take up the strands of their lives. They married, established careers, became fathers and grandfathers, rarely speaking of their time in the Far East which had robbed them of the prime years of their youth. A younger generation which has only ever lived in peace would never truly understand what they went through in war. Perhaps the words of this prayer, said often by Far East POWs during Remembrance Services, best expresses their feelings:

> *We who are left grow old with the years*
> *Remembering the heartache, the pain and the tears,*
> *Hoping and praying that never again*
> *Will man sink to such sorrow and shame.*
> *The price that we paid we will always remember*
> *Every day, every month — not just in November.*

Margaret

Margaret was just eighteen when she first got married. She left the home of her strictly Methodist adoptive parents in which cuddles were rare and emotions kept tightly under control – and walked down the aisle totally in love with the idea of having a husband, home and family of her own. The man she married was kind and well-meaning, older than her by four years, and yet two years on, after the birth of their first daughter, Jemma, Margaret had grown up fast, while her husband still seemed very young. By the time their second daughter, Diane, arrived eighteen months later, the gap in the couple's maturity had widened, until they simply drifted apart. No great trauma, no hard feelings, but it left Margaret, at the age of twenty-two, with the daunting responsibility of two small children to bring up on her own.

Very occasionally, she was able to take a few hours out for her own social life and within the year it was at a Singles Club that she met the man with whom she was to share her life. Bill quite literally swept her off her feet. She fell instantly in love with him even though he was eight years older than her. Best of all was the fact that from the start he got on brilliantly with her two daughters, which wasn't surprising once she knew he worked professionally with children. He was solid and caring, able to provide for Margaret everything she felt she had lacked not only in her first marriage, but in her childhood. He surrounded the family with love and security, insisting that she need never look at anyone else because within their own tight unit, both children and adults had everything they required.

Bill felt it best that the girls didn't keep up contact with their real father, because it might confuse them, and Margaret was happy to go along with that arrangement as her relationship with Bill became more established, and they set up home together. After a couple of years, once Margaret and Bill were married, Jemma and Diane asked if they could call their stepfather 'dad' – and the family were secure in the knowledge that they were settled and contented for life.

They started with very little, living in a council flat with no garden on an estate where the police would constantly be turning up to arrest one neighbour or another, but Bill and Margaret worked together from home to build a business which enabled them to claw their way up and out. After years of hard work during which the couple were constantly in each other's company day and night, Margaret looked back to think how lucky she was to have been given a second chance, by finding a man with whom she was ecstatically happy. They added to their family with a son of their own, who was born ten years after the younger of his two big sisters.

Even when they'd been together more than fifteen years, Bill and Margaret would relish the fact that their relationship had never become simply a habit, as they were still in love and totally happy in each other's company. They did everything together – mostly because Bill insisted on it. That occasionally led to conflict when his jealousy not just for his wife, but for their daughters too, seemed over-protective and even downright unreasonable. 'Sometimes,' recalls Margaret, 'he would manipulate a situation that was entirely wrong, so that I'd have to spend the next three weeks trying to explain that his accusations were untrue. He would say that I'd been looking at someone in a way which must mean I was having an affair. I was happy to reassure him though, because I believed his jealousy stemmed from the experience of his own parents' divorce which left him with a deep mistrust of women. I felt it was my mission to support him and give him confidence, by putting his feelings before mine so that he'd never have cause to feel jealous.'

The one thing Margaret didn't worry about was the possibility of Bill being attracted to other women. In twenty-three years, she never had even the slightest suspicion that he was looking elsewhere. After all, because Bill preferred his family to keep to themselves, they never socialized, and therefore had few friends. 'He would say, "Why do we need other people, when we've got each other?" – and I didn't mind,' remembers Margaret. 'I knew it was a very tight, controlled environment, but because I felt all encompassed by a man who appeared to live and breathe for me, well, what more could I want?'

Certainly their children seemed happy enough, even though Bill always said that he was one of those people 'who didn't appreciate children'. 'Once I got to know him better,' says Margaret, 'I began to realize that he didn't particularly like children, which was odd when I think that he was working with children when we first met. But he never played with our youngsters, nor showed much interest in them. He would never take them out on his own either, and on the few occasions when we all went out together as a family, he was plainly not very keen about it. At first, I didn't mind his lack of attention towards the girls, especially as it meant that he didn't interfere with my way of discipline, but in time he became quite insistent about the children keeping out of his way, and dogmatic about what he expected of them. We would all do exactly what he told us to do. He was adamant that the children completed certain tasks. There was no argument about it. I remember once that he ruled that they couldn't go out until they'd cleaned the windows. The windows didn't need cleaning, but he insisted all the same. Gemma, by this time, was an excellent student at school, while Diane was much more gregarious, a fun-loving girl. Neither of them ever said a bad word against Bill, and were always very loyal, good and obedient. It was quite clear that they loved him dearly, which pleased me because I loved him very much too.

'Bill ordered that boyfriends were strictly forbidden for our girls, and became completely inflexible about the time they should be home, and their general behaviour. I suppose to a degree I understood, because I didn't like the thought of the girls wandering the streets late at night either, but I did think they deserved to have fun as teenagers too. It caused quite a bit of conflict at the time. In the end, at the ages of eighteen and twenty, the two girls decided to leave home together and move into a flat just round the corner. Bill didn't want them to go, and when they did, he was so indignant at being disobeyed that he forbade them to come back home, or even visit. If they left home, he said, then that was it. What he didn't realize, and I never let him know, was that because they lived quite nearby, I would take my son to school every morning, then nip round to their flat to take them a few groceries, and make sure they were all right. Any mum would do the same. It was good to see how happy they were, although I was very sad that for two years or so, he never allowed them to come back into our home. Actually, the house seemed really empty to me after the girls left, although I knew that all children must fly the nest. I just wish I could have visited them openly.'

It wasn't long before the girls had not only found partners, but decided they wanted to get married. It was the younger daughter, Diane, who made the announcement first, and Bill was vitriolic. He most certainly didn't approve of her choice of husband, and made it clear that Margaret was not to get involved in the wedding in any way. 'It was most distressing,' says Margaret. 'Like any mother I would have loved to have helped her with the arrangements, the dresses, catering, and so on, but Bill flatly forbade me. In the end, our son, Neil, and I crept into the back of the church so that we could watch her actually getting married. I was so thrilled to see that the church was packed with Diane's friends. Of course, she didn't think I would be coming, but Chinese Whispers went round the place so that she was aware that Neil and I were there in the end. I know she was only twenty, and of course she could have been making a dreadful mistake, but as it turns out, she wasn't. Her husband is a lovely man, and they've been together for years now. They've got two gorgeous children, Barney and Katie, and the whole family is really happy.

'We went through the same traumatic time when Jemma decided, after years of living with her fiancé, that they wanted to get married. And they too are still happily together today, with their two young sons, Tom and Bobby.

'Bill continued to be very possessive about me, and intensely jealous of any time I spent with my daughters. Often, they would ring me up on a Saturday morning to ask if I fancied going shopping with them. Bill would be furious at the idea that he would have to stay on his own in the house while I was out with them. His attitude was, "Well, if you want to go shopping, we'll *both* go shopping. If there's something you want, I'll buy it for you." In the end, I began to wonder if it was really important to stand up to him, when it was much simpler just to keep the peace — so usually I gave in and stayed at home.'

By the time Neil was sixteen, Bill and Margaret had been running their business for about twenty years. For five years, Margaret had also been running the retail shop they had set up when the recession hit their other business badly. They had started off working in the shop together, but after six months Bill grew bored with it, and Margaret was left to man the shop alone, going in at nine each morning, and coming home at five every night. She was quite concerned by the fact that although by this time Bill was prepared to tolerate visits by the girls and their families, neither Jemma nor Diane had been to their house for several months, even over the Christmas period. No explanation had been given. In fact, the girls had been very evasive whenever she tried to talk to them about the distance they were keeping.

One day while she was at the shop, Margaret was surprised to see Diane and Jemma arrive without their children. Because a carpet fitter was working in the shop that morning, conversation was stilted at first as they sat around making small talk. It was clear that the girls were on edge because they had something difficult to say. Margaret sat there with her arms folded, thinking that they'd come to explain why they'd been staying away, and when the carpet fitter finally left, they began. What they told her changed her life for ever.

'They told me that practically from the moment we had moved in with Bill, when they were no more than four and six years old, he had sexually abused them. He threatened them that if they ever told anyone, they would be taken away because no one would believe them. Who would believe a child? Later he told them that if either of them told, then they or I would be killed. Children understand fear. It's what keeps them alive.

'At first, they had simply done what they were told. They didn't understand that it was wrong. They didn't know. Children don't. If you tell a child to clean their teeth with a lump of coal, that's what they'll do. He had abused them both separately and together. It happened three or four times a week for years and years and years, not stopping until they were going through puberty. He didn't want young women. He had no interest in them if they were no longer children. And worst of all, I discovered that he even abused them when I was actually in the house. I would be washing up or cooking a meal in the kitchen, upstairs making beds, outside pegging up washing. I'd be having a bath, or an early night. I'd be sewing curtains in another room ... There are so many times in family life when you're not actually in the room with everyone else. I found myself looking back over every second of those twenty-three years, and seeing it from a different perspective.

'And the moment they told me, I knew it was true. I was in total shock, but I believed them. Since then I've wondered why I believed them so emphatically. I knew he was a cruel man. Now I could see that what mattered to him was having power. He ruled them with fear. They reacted by trying to protect me, and each other. And yet, I know they loved him. If you have a dog that you kick ten times a day, it will still love you. There's nothing more loyal than an abused dog.

'They had only decided to tell me then, after all those years, because they recognized that he was starting to "groom" my little granddaughter, Katie. They instantly knew the signs. I now know that this is something paedophiles do. They identify a vulnerable child – and let's face it, all children are vulnerable, especially if they're only two years old – and they focus attention on them. It can be done very quickly, or it can take months and months. It depends on the cleverness of the paedophile, and the vulnerability of the child – and a paedophile can walk into a room and immediately pick out the most vulnerable child.

'When my daughter explained to me how she had recognized the way in which Bill was behaving towards Katie, I immediately knew it was true. I remembered the occasion so clearly myself, even though I didn't understand it at the time. Usually, he would say, "Not those bloody kids again, can't we have a bit of peace? Why don't you take your children home?" But on that occasion, even I had noticed that he was being very sweet to Katie, paying her particular attention. My daughter just scooped her two children up, left the house without an explanation, and never returned.

'Jemma, Diane and I sat there in the shop, crying and hugging for hours. I realized that they had been terrified I wasn't going to believe them — that I might just accuse them of lying, and go home to play happy families again. But I didn't think of doing that for a moment, not a single second.

'We realized it was getting towards my normal going-home time. Somehow I felt that I could sort this out. I wasn't clear what I was going to do, but I knew I had to go home because my son was there. Besides, I needed some space to think. We had two businesses that were very complex. We had a home and our son, Neil. The whole twenty-three years of our life together was very firmly built. I had to go back and decide what best to do. I told them not to ring me or come round to the house for a few days.

'That evening is very vivid in my mind, because I spent it seeming absolutely normal, but never actually looking at him. We had conversations, but I couldn't look him in the eye. We sat in the lounge watching television, eating pizza and chips, and I couldn't physically swallow. I wasn't crying, but I couldn't swallow. Then I went to bed as normal — until he got in the other side, and I simply got out and sat up in the chair all night, awake. That was a Friday, with the weekend ahead. I went out at eight o'clock the next morning to my daughter's, and didn't come back until three o'clock the following day. In twenty-three years, I'd never done anything like that — *and he didn't say a word*. This man who had always been so possessive and jealous about me, didn't react at all. He knew. He *knew!* I couldn't believe he had nothing to say after twenty-three years. Not a word, not a single word. Not even, "Where have you been?" I didn't expect any kindness. I just thought I would come home one night during that week, and find the house smashed to bits, or that he'd be ranting, raving and screaming, because that was his nature. He had always been emotionally and verbally violent towards us, and when all this came out, I honestly feared for my life. In fact, I got in touch with the police and without saying who I was, or being too specific about what had happened, I tried to tell them that I thought I and my family were going to be killed. Of course, because I was too afraid to give them my name, they just thought I was a nutcase. I wish I could have been more honest with them, but because the girls were over the age of eighteen, it had to be their decision, rather than mine, to report his abuse of them to the police – and neither of them felt strong enough to go through that. Besides, they loved him. This was the man they had called "Dad" for years. Love and hatred are so close, just like respect and abhorrence. We all knew enough to realize that the court system can be very abusive. How could I ask my children to go through an abusive situation all over again?

'I kept coming home for the first few days, because I had to find a way of getting my son out. In the end, we decided that Diane should be the one to tell Neil. We managed to get him round to her house – and he was just devastated. From then on, both of us moved in with Diane rather than stay at the house with him there.

'We knew Bill had to be challenged with the truth, and perhaps shamed into leaving the house, and our lives, but we couldn't do that ourselves. Finally, we found a colleague who was a private investigator, who worked with an independent witness to take statements from the girls. I had to go back to the house to let the two men in when they arrived to confront my husband. I couldn't help myself creeping down the stairs to listen for a minute or two at the door, then I'd run up again and hide. Some of the things I overheard, though, were just unbelievable. When he heard the charges and the statements, he simply replied, "Oh well, I can explain this. My wife's having an affair, and she wants out of this marriage, but she had to blame it on me. The girls have got together with her, and dreamt up this elaborate story just so that she can get a divorce. That's what she's like!" One minute he was reasoning along those lines, the next he'd be angry, indignant and bolshy, asking them who the hell they thought they were. But then, you've got to remember that he was a man who knew exactly what he'd done, and was trying to act innocent. He would never admit guilt. I now know that paedophiles rarely do. Like so many of them, he is a very skilled manipulator with years and years of practice behind him. He was confident that the girls loved him too much to report him to the police, so he felt reasonably safe.

'He denied it all, and refused to leave. That left Neil and me living out of suitcases in my daughter's house, while he stayed perfectly comfortable at home. Eventually, enough was enough. We decided that if he wouldn't leave the house, then the house would have to leave him! Every day when he was out, we let ourselves in and removed bits and pieces we knew he needed. Gradually we got more confident. After three or four days, we were taking away knives and forks, cups and saucers, plates, food, bedding, fires, the telephone, computer, even the kettle. It would have been no good him changing the locks, because it was my home too, and I would have just broken in. Finally, when I took his beloved toolkit, he slunk off and disappeared like a slug into the night. We had no idea where he'd gone, but it was such a relief to know that he was out of the area, so that I could walk down the street and not be afraid of bumping into him, or of him approaching my children.

'I didn't want to move back into that house, but really there was no alternative. My son was at college studying for his GCSEs, and in spite of everything, the family had to keep going. Whenever we had gone to the house to take things away, we had just thrown whatever we took into boxes in the back of the car — so when it came to moving back in, I had boxes everywhere. Even now I haven't got round to sorting some of them out.

'And of course, the business was in total chaos. I did return to the shop in zombie mode for four months, but I can't remember anything about it. I have no recollection of what happened business-wise. I know there was a lot of mail that wasn't opened. If people got in touch to say "I want this, I need that, you promised me this", I simply didn't reply. And because it was a limited company, there were legal implications of me doing one thing or another – so I did nothing.

'That time is just a blur now really – so many thoughts going round my head. I spent twenty-six hours a day trying to work out *why*. Now I know it's not possible for any normal person to understand. Only a paedophile can have any idea how a fully grown man in his mid-thirties can abuse, molest and rape a little child day after day for years and years. What can you say? What words are there? I couldn't understand how he could live with what he'd done. I thought he would kill himself, because if I knew I had done something as abhorrent as that, I would have to commit suicide. But he felt no guilt. More than that, when I moved back into the house, we discovered evidence of sites he had downloaded on to the computer – and you must remember that he was a very computer-literate man. Within the first few days of him realizing that I knew the truth, he had accessed information about the Children's Act, and court procedures which he thought he might need to know. He wanted to be sure of his rights – and how to behave. He had actually searched for information on how to appear depressed, as that would be mitigating evidence if he was charged.

'Three or four months later, he rang to tell me that everything I needed to know would be in the divorce papers. Oddly enough that was the first time I had considered the idea of divorce. I suppose I hadn't been thinking logically enough before. He was divorcing me on the grounds of *my* unreasonable behaviour! I couldn't believe my ears. I wanted to contest those grounds, but I wasn't granted Legal

Aid to do that. I soon discovered anyway that nowadays you can't really contest a divorce. If one party wants the split, then there will be a divorce. However, I didn't intend to take the situation lying down. If I couldn't expose his behaviour by contesting our divorce, then I decided to fight him over the financial settlement. I went to see several solicitors, but I was frankly amazed by the reaction I got from some of them. One even thought I should be paying him maintenance! I remember saying to him, "Listen, and watch my lips — I am *not* paying maintenance to that man, *no!*" The solicitor mumbled away about how if the court says I have pay, I'll just have to — and I said, "You're not listening to me. I would sooner go to prison than pay a penny to that man." And I sacked him.

'It was around that time that I decided that if nobody would help me, and nothing was going to be done to expose John, then I would have to do it myself. By that time, I knew where he was living, at the other end of the country. I had 500 leaflets printed up with a picture of him, and a message which warned mothers in the area that a paedophile was living near them and their children. Then I got into the car and drove for hours through the night to the place where I knew he was. I had never driven anything like that distance before, so it felt like a really scary adventure when I set off at eleven o'clock at night. By six in the morning, I had distributed 350 posters around the town, sticking posters on café windows, children's playgrounds, shop fronts, lamp posts — anywhere flat enough to take a poster. I would have done the other 150, but I was arrested. Two police cars, a police wagon and a motorbike all turned up to arrest me, because they'd had a complaint that I was distributing obscene literature! I was absolutely terrified, but I did try to explain that the word "paedophile" appeared in the Oxford English Dictionary so how could it possibly be "obscene"? They didn't agree, so they made a roadside arrest with the charge of causing an affray and breach of the peace. In fact, I was given three minutes to get out of town —

almost as if it was a Wild West movie! I left as fast as I could, driving for eight hours to get back home – and then I had to wait six weeks to see if they planned to prosecute me.

'The police apparently talked to Bill, and said that they found him "a most charming man". I suggested that they talk to their own Child Protection Unit to find out how manipulative and plausible paedophiles are. Then they phoned me to say that if my daughter would go to the police to make a *criminal* charge against him, they would drop the case against me. How could I ask my daughters to go through that? Of course I couldn't. My daughters both feel they'd never be strong enough to make a criminal charge against him. But eventually the police did drop the case against me, and apart from an official warning from my local police station, that was it – except for the phone call I had from Bill suggesting that we went away for the weekend to "sort this out", as he thought he could "talk some sense into me". You can guess my reaction to that . . .

'Anyway, before the divorce could be finalized, I decided that I would make a point of contesting the usual fifty-fifty split of assets. I was refused Legal Aid on that as well, so I went to the Legal Aid tribunal to put my case. Five people were sitting behind a great big intimidating table, and little me had to walk five miles down the room to sit in a lonely little chair and explain why that man should not be allowed to take a single penny away from my family, when he had already taken more than enough. I argued the case for Legal Aid so that I could bring, for the very first time as it turned out, a *civil* case where the perpetrator is a step-father who has abused the children in his care. Thank God that tribunal supported me – and that led to four days in a civil court, where the man who had been my husband and I sat side by side around a table in front of a judge for a proper child abuse hearing. The findings of that court would decide if there was just cause to stop him benefiting from the assets of the family business.

'I'll never forget how gruelling those four days were for me, and my daughters who found the courage to come and support me. We all faced a full cross-examination, table banging, shouting – the lot – just as you see on television. "I put it to you … I suggest that …" I remember the barrister asking my daughter, "If it was so awful, why did you get into bed with your father?" – and she replied in a tiny whisper which sounded just like the six year old she had been at the time, "Because he told me to." It was dreadful, humiliating, abusive, traumatic – and after our four days of evidence, my husband spoke for just five minutes. In the end, the judge's summing-up made it clear that he found our evidence overwhelmingly compelling, and that because in his opinion, my husband had abused my children, I should be awarded all assets. That was a precedent. It had never happened before, but because of our case, that door is now open to other mothers in my position.'

That civil action was successful, but so traumatic that Margaret's daughters felt more strongly than ever that they couldn't face the prospect of bringing police charges against the man they thought of as their father. Margaret not only sympathizes with their feelings, but understands their reaction. 'The trouble with children who have been abused is that they have a basic need to survive at all costs. Some children don't. Some die, or commit suicide. I am very fortunate that my children are survivors, very strong people, and they only went through that civil court for my sake. In their minds, it was for me – not them. It wasn't anything to do with them. It wasn't anything to do with him. It was for me. If they went to the police, it would be for them, and they would have to face it themselves then – and they can't do that. What I do know is that my daughters and I are closer than ever now. We're never afraid of saying what we feel. We have no secrets. Everything is on the table, warts and all, where in the past we may have chosen to keep our thoughts to ourselves in case we hurt or upset someone. If there's a problem, then we talk about it openly. And we all know that absolutely no matter what, nothing, *nothing*, will separate the bond that we share.

'They understand that one of the things I'll never be able to come to terms with is that throughout all those years, I didn't know. I didn't see — and they couldn't tell me. The most important thing in my life was my family, and keeping them happy, healthy and safe. You don't let your children play in the road. You don't let them wander off to rubbish dumps or empty houses. You teach them not speak to strangers. I wouldn't let them ride their bikes without their cycling proficiency training. And all the time, they were being abused in their own home. Home is where they're supposed to be safe, isn't it? Oh, I know that people keep telling me it's not my fault, I simply could not have known, it's not my responsibility — but frankly to me they are just words.

'Part of the pain is not just that my children were abused and all the ramifications of that, but that on a very personal level I have lost twenty-three years of my life. It's like a death, but worse in some ways because with a death, someone can put their arms around you and say how dreadful that loss is. But with this, you can tell no one. No one can identify with your pain. The knowledge of what's happened to you and your children is too awful to share. You feel as if people are looking at you as if you must have known what was going on — but I just didn't. So it's worse than dealing with bereavement. You have the same physical loss of the person you have loved for years not being there. In one moment, you're catapulted from being happy and in love — to nothing. And it's not possible to turn off your feelings like a light switch, even when you have to accept that for twenty-three years you have lived with and loved a monster who was actually abusing your trust, your love, your very body. We shared a bed, we made love — and all the time he was raping my children. He abused us all. I now believe that right back at the beginning when we first met, he picked my daughters first, and then manipulated me. The moment he saw my girls very early on in our relationship, he chose them. I was a by-product, a secondary consideration. We met at a Singles Club. Single mothers are the most vulnerable, often living on a low income, and alone with their children. In fact, many paedophiles find their victims through Lonely Hearts Clubs or newspaper columns. After all, we're like cattle in a meat market there, aren't we? They have the pick of the bunch. All those lovely children. I'm sorry if I sound cynical, but I've learned so much about paedophiles since I discovered all this. I remember thinking this couldn't be happening to us. We were a nice, educated, successful middle-class family. I remember walking around for three or four months with my head in my hands, thinking this couldn't be happening because we were too "nice". But things aren't always what they seem – and you never really know anyone. I lived with that man for nearly a quarter of a century, and didn't know him at all.

'I know that he is now approaching sixty, and he will be doing it again. He has survived for sixty years as a paedophile. He has never had a conviction, and he never will unless somebody comes forward who is brave enough to stand up to him – and victims seldom find enough strength and courage to do that. I understand that paedophiles have often been abused themselves, and have grown up with a warped personality deficiency where they have no responsibility. They take no responsibility for their action. And they need a power kick. The power is more important than the sex. They say things like, "Well, she provoked me. She tantalized me. She was asking for it. She needed to be shown what sex is. It was my duty to show her what sex is." It's as if they feel it's their right to do whatever they want to that child, no question about it – just as it's your right to use your hoover anyway you choose to. It's yours to do what you like with. You can kick it to bits if you want to. No matter that the child may only be eight years old...

'They have power over everything they come into contact with – the home, the family, the wife, their friends, their business. They're bullies at work. They're people in positions of power. They might be school teachers who tell children what to do. They're sometimes doctors, judges, barristers, solicitors, accountants, vicars – all people who tell others what to do, who are looked up to and respected. It's the power that matters.

'So yes, I do worry about what he's up to now. Leopards don't change their spots – it's the nature of the beast. He won't survive without children. That's his power thing. That's what he is. He was a paedophile before I met him, and he's still a paedophile now.

'But one thing that has come out of this is that I now know how strong I am. Like any woman in an abusive relationship, I had always had to be strong because my role was to keep the peace with a volatile partner. To protect my children from violence and anger was always hard work, so I knew I had that sort of strength. But to fight back and maintain my own integrity has taken every ounce of that strength. One of the very positive outcomes of my experience is that I've started a self-help group for other mothers of children who have been sexually abused. Through groups like ours I would like to see a future where this subject is much more open, where both children and mothers have the freedom to speak, be heard and supported, and most of all, believed. We have developed a very strong group here who are managing to change local opinion quite substantially. We have talked to other women's groups, to probation workers, prison officers and social services – because shared knowledge, education, openness are all the keys to protecting future generations of children. One thing that's got to change is the attitude of some GPs, and their lack of knowledge. Sometimes when a mother plucks up the courage to go to the doctor because she's not sleeping or thinking straight because of the discovery she's made, the reaction of some doctors is still, "Well, you can imagine all sorts of things, can't you?" That's still happening — and only practical knowledge and education are going to change that. We've got to change the pattern. There is no question about it. We are living in a society that cares more for animals than our own children. We're outraged if a poor dolphin gets washed up on the beach — we'll move heaven and earth to get it back into the sea. We're appalled if someone kicks their dog to death. But what about our children? These abused children are the adults of tomorrow. There are hundreds of adults walking around who are victims of what happened to them in their childhood.

'I remember myself ten years ago, a mother in a nice, middle-class family. If I saw something distasteful in the paper, I would flick over the page and ignore it because it didn't affect me. But then, nor did safe sex ten years ago. Now we're all aware of the dangers of Aids, and we walk around with our ribbon, and talk to our children openly about having safe sex. If we could do it with Aids, then we have to be equally open about child abuse if we want to change attitudes and the threat to our children. In ten years' time, providing the authorities know the signs and what to look for, they can disseminate information so that it's accessible to individuals like me who have worries and suspicions.

'It was only a year ago that I became aware of what had been happening in my own family. It's too late for me, twenty years too late for my kids. But it's not too late for other children, other mothers — and from now on, with every breath in my body, I'm going to work to make sure that future generations are protected from these monsters who prey on young bodies, and steal their childhood.'

Andrew

I can think of no one I have ever met in my life who touched me more than Andrew Allam. His story – the hardship, the poverty, the longing, the persecution, the salvation – and the lessons we could all learn from him will stay with me for ever. Here in Great Britain, we are comfortable and secure enough to grumble about our lot. In Southern Sudan, where Andrew was born in 1968, to profess your faith, to argue with government officials, to be hungry enough for food, water or education to be on the point of desperation – any of these could be a death sentence.

Andrew was the second son in a family of five boys. None of them knew their father, and Andrew could never really say he was close to his mother either. It was his grandmother for whom he felt most affection – so much so that at the age of seven, he decided to leave his home in Torit, the biggest town in that Eastern Equatorial area of Southern Sudan, to go and live with his grandmother three miles away. There he settled down on her smallholding, with her goats and sheep, her small garden where they grew mangoes, guava and papaya, and any crops such as maize and sorghum which they could manage. Life was a struggle for the elderly lady and her small grandson, every day a fight for survival. Andrew would go to market to try and sell fruit, hoping to make enough money to buy salt, sugar and other items they couldn't grow themselves. Worst of all were the rainy months between July and September leading up to the harvest, when food was sometimes desperately short. In spite of being young in years, Andrew was the man of the household, cultivating the land, taking the livestock out into the bush until about five o'clock every day when he would bring them back home and milk them. Grandmother would be cooking, so that the two of them ended the day together with only each other for company.

For a lively youngster, it was a solitary life. Andrew amused himself by creating playthings out of whatever he found around him. From the clay at his feet he would make a model bull. And when he looked up to the sky, he would often see aeroplanes on their way from Ethiopia or Uganda. He'd never seen a plane closer than half a mile above him, but he still managed to copy its shape into a treasured toy.

Most of the time, Andrew didn't bother to wear clothes. They were a luxury kept only for high days and holidays. Once a year at Christmas, if he had really been a good boy and worked hard on the farm, his grandmother would buy him a few items of clothing – perhaps a pair of sandals, shorts or a T-shirt. Whatever it was, he knew he had to wear it for twelve months, washing it out at night, and putting it on again in the morning. Busy on the farm, and out in the bush taking care of the animals, hardly warranted the wearing of precious clothes – so more often than not, he left them at home.

What Andrew hungered for mostly was not food, but education. Even if his grandmother could spare the money needed to buy schooling, she could not spare him from his responsibilities on the farm. Day after day, Andrew would watch with longing as other boys walked through the village on their way to school. He knew that an education was the only route towards improving not just his own chances, but those of his family. Eventually, at the age of nine, his desperation made him daring. Without his grandmother's knowledge, he started saving a few coins in an old milk can each week from the groceries he took to market. When he had enough, he took himself off to primary school, making up for his late start by working with great enthusiasm in the hope that he would catch up with the other pupils. All his grandmother saw was that he left with the lifestock in the morning for a day in the bush. What she didn't know was that he was leaving them to fend for themselves while he raced away to sit at his desk. Before going home time, he would tell his teacher he had to rush back to collect his animals. It wasn't until a year later when he decided he'd like to join the seminary, in other words, train to be a priest, that he finally had to tell his grandmother the truth.

She was angry at first, to think that he had betrayed her trust. They both knew she needed him to run the farm, although his devotion to their Catholic faith was something they both shared. Every evening, Andrew would hear her praying in what he thought was 'the language of God', which he later realized was Latin. In their area of Southern Sudan, unlike the Muslim North, most people were Christian – some Presbyterian, some Anglican, but mostly Catholic. Walking the few miles to the Mission with his grandmother was a regular trip for the young boy, instilling in him a deep faith from which he has drawn strength and resilience during the most turbulent times of his life. His belief in God stemmed not from doctrine, but from long hours of sitting in the bush, thinking about what he saw around him. 'I could just sit,' he says, 'and everything I saw was a testimony to God who made it. The land is God itself. I sat under the sky, heard the birds singing, ran my fingers through the grass, felt the wind on my face, and felt not only close to the earth, but close to God who created it. Early in the morning, I would look across the landscape after milking the animals, and thank God for this land which kept us alive. It was everything. He was everything. I was filled with a sense of respect and belonging. My only friends were the animals, my grandmother – and God. I used to talk to God, not formal prayers, but share my thoughts with Him. I would thank Him for all His blessings, and ask for help and guidance. I never wanted to go to confession at the Mission, because if I thought I had done something wrong, I would rather talk to God personally and ask for forgiveness, than ask a priest, who is only another man, to intervene on my behalf.

'But even at the age of ten, I recognized that I would find great fulfilment in becoming a priest myself. This was partly out of my deep commitment to faith, and partly, if I'm honest, because priests seemed to command not only respect in the district, but a very comfortable lifestyle. Apart from that, I come from the Lotuka tribe, a warrior tribe. The initiation ceremony as you become a man is that you drink fresh blood mixed with milk. They would go raiding, stealing cows and killing innocent people, if they got in the way. If I became a priest, I could see a world where I could change that, help them to understand that there is more to life than pagan traditions like theirs.'

The Lotuka, like so many other tribes, had accepted the Catholic faith years before because schooling and food were part of the benefits of conversion. However, as the Muslim government in the north of the country became more fundamentalist, it became more and more difficult for the southerners to remain Christian. It was getting to the point where jobs, schooling and even food were only available to Muslims. Not much later, sharia, Islamic law, was enforced across the Sudan. After that, anyone caught stealing would have their right hand cut off. If you were found drinking or merely possessing alcohol, you would be publicly flogged, and a woman caught wearing a short skirt would be flogged and thrown to her death. The stench of fear was taking grip on the country, where a careless comment could be reported by neighbours betraying other neighbours.

The year that Andrew was twelve, there was a dreadful drought which killed all their livestock, devastating their meagre crop to the extent that the farm could no longer sustain two people. The boy walked back to Torit to stay again with his mother and brothers, getting himself a cleaning and packing job so that he could send a few coins back to his grandmother, and carry on with his schooling.

By the time he was fourteen, civil war was raging around him. The Sudan People's Liberation Army, the SPLA, were mainly Christians fighting for the autonomy of southern Sudan, and the freedom to follow their faith. The Muslim government made the decision to 'protect' Torit from the rebels, which meant that the town was under siege, with the Christian SPLA surrounding the outside as it tried to rescue the Christian community from official Muslim control. Schools were shut, food was scarce and Torit was dying, starving to death. 'Only the big fish could get food, but the tiny fish, we found that we were eating ourselves. Small fish were betraying others so that they would be given food. So I told my grandmother that I was going to take her to Juba, the capital city of southern Sudan. My mother had already made her way there, so we decided to go, my nine-year-old niece, Ehure, my grandmother and I.

'There were many civilians making that journey, all under the protection of the government. It was eighty-four miles from Torit to Juba, so would take us three days. But in order to get there, we had to drive through the SPLA, who were Christians like us but who only saw us as a government convoy and, therefore, the enemy. Hundreds of innocent people were simply victims, caught in the crossfire. There were eight or nine trucks, each holding a hundred people or so. Mostly I just walked alongside the trucks with the other young people, but my grandmother was on board because she couldn't walk.

'There was no food or water, none at all. The only way we could survive was to drink each other's urine. When it was your turn to pee, I would ask you if I could please drink your urine because it would be edible in my system, and then when my time came, I would also pee, and you would drink mine. That is how we stayed alive.

'The third day was the worst. Once again we were ambushed – bullets everywhere. You just had to fall flat or you'd get a bullet in your back. My grandmother was still on the lorry, because she couldn't get down. It was terrifying for her, because she was a sitting target, waiting to be shot. Eventually, our attackers moved off, and we started walking again, with about ten or eleven miles left to reach Juba. We were dying of thirst, so when we came across a hand pump, my niece, who had refused to drink urine, was so desperate that she, and several others, just rushed towards it. I yelled at her not to go, but it was too late! The pump was surrounded by anti-personnel landmines. All we heard were the explosions – doof, doof, doof ... Nine people were lost in those moments ... and Ehure, poor Ehure ... she was blown to pieces, her legs torn away from her. I ran over to her to scoop her into my arms. She was asking for water, just water – and surely, as water is life, it should be a gift to everyone? All around us people were praying in their own language, clutching their loved ones to them. But what could we do? We were so weak, really weak. We didn't even have the strength to bury them. And so we left them. We had to. The last word Ehure said to me was to ask me to cover her. So I covered her with some leaves and left her there for the vultures to eat. I couldn't tell my grandmother what had happened to her. The grief would have killed her.'

But when Andrew got to Juba, it offered little more than Torit. His mother's house had become home to an extended family with relatives from far and wide coming to stay. If they were lucky, they would eat once a day. Sometimes, they were unlucky. It didn't take him long to realize that there was no future for him in Juba. Khartoum was the answer. But Khartoum was not only in the north and the fundamentalist Muslim government stronghold, it was also more than four thousand miles away. For a fourteen-year-old lad from Juba with no money and no transport, making the decision to leave his homeland was hard enough. Getting there was practically impossible.

In the end, desperation and sheer cheek paid off. Andrew knew that cargo planes arrived bringing food to Juba from Khartoum, returning later with coffee beans from the south that were needed in the north. He managed to hide himself inside a bag of beans, almost suffocating as the guards checked and investigated the cargo. He stayed motionless inside the bag for more than three hours in temperatures above 40 degrees – until, once the plane was airborne, he staggered out. The guards were furious with him, demanding to know what he was doing there, and how he got inside. 'I just told them that I was really very sorry, but that I had to get to Khartoum and couldn't think of another way. They threw me out at Khartoum – and I discovered a world I'd never even dreamed of. I didn't know anyone there, and I wandered around lost and alone at first. Then I saw a Sudanese man who was obviously from the south and therefore probably a Christian. I plucked up courage to talk to him and tell him my story. He took pity on me, and invited me to go home with him – that's if you could call a house made of boxes home.'

That man's kindness was a start for Andrew, who eventually managed to get himself enrolled in one of the few schools funded by Western governments to aid the displaced people of southern

Sudan. Getting a job posed a different problem. Jobs were only given to Muslims, and many southerners had chosen to adopt the Muslim faith simply to get work, food and a home for their families. 'James became Juma,' explains Andrew, 'and every Friday they would go to the mosque. They were getting deep into Arabic and the Islamic system – and they would say to me that if I wanted to feed and educate myself, why didn't I join them? But for me that was impossible. My Christian faith was the basis of my life. It was my foundation, and nothing would rock me from it. They could shake me, tempt me, but you have to stand up for what you believe in. I was born a Christian. I would die a Christian.'

A few years later, Andrew was finishing his senior leaving certificate – and already married. In their culture, marriage required no formal ceremony or certificate, but the simple approval of all interested friends and family. Certainly Andrew and Anna were very much in love. She was younger than him, only sixteen years old, and pregnant. By this time, Andrew had become very outspoken in his opinions about the Muslim government, until eventually his colleagues at school elected him to become Chairman of the Student Union. 'I spoke up for their rights,' he says, 'and the allowances which should have been theirs. Money was sent for them by the Western governments which the Muslim government were spending instead on guns and ammunitions so that they could go and kill our mothers and sisters in the south. I spoke out – and before I knew it, I was in prison.'

For three days, he endured the most inhuman ordeal of beatings and torture. 'I was terrified,' he recalls, 'especially the first day when I didn't know what was going to happen. I soon found out. Every morning they used to come. They would strip me and the other prisoners, and when we were all naked, pour cold water over us, then bring electric wires and turn on the current. They put them all over my body, even on my penis, and deep under my finger and toe nails until in the end all my nails fell off. They would beat me, leave, then come back later to torture and beat me again before they tried once more to interrogate me. Was I working with the rebels? Why was I so outspoken against the government if I wasn't a rebel sympathizer? I told them that I was simply speaking on behalf of my fellow students. The money was ours by right. It was not fair that we weren't given our proper allowances. I was simply asking for what was rightfully ours.

'Strangely enough, one of the other men being beaten was a Muslim. I don't know what had happened to him, or what he did. I was suspicious of him because he was in my cell, and I wondered if he was trying to get information out of me. So I didn't respond much, but I shall never forget what he said to me. He said that had I been a Muslim, they would have let me go. The problem was that I was a Christian, and I would not renounce my faith. And then he said that he thought my God was very powerful, and that if I really did have faith in Jesus Christ, then go for it, stick to what you believe, take the torture! I remember thinking of what Barrabas said to Jesus when they were being crucified, when Christ was being tortured for his faith, and thinking that the situation was the same. I looked at the Muslim, and thanked him. I shall never forget that. I believe that God can let you fall into the hands of your enemy where they can break your flesh – but to break your spirit, your belief, God will not allow that.

'They came again on the last day. They beat me like a balloon, kicked me like a football. Finally, I blacked out completely. I was dimly aware of being put on the back of a truck and when I woke up, probably about four o'clock in the morning, I had no idea where I was. I started staggering around, realizing that I had been thrown out on to a rubbish dump, perhaps because they thought I was dead. Then I saw an Arab, obviously a Muslim – and not all Muslims are bad any more than all Christians are good, because that man took pity on me. I must have looked almost dead, with no clothes at all, battered, swollen and bleeding. He asked me what I was doing there, and when I said I didn't know, he asked where I lived. He was delivering meat to the stores, and he put me in his truck and took me back to the area I knew.

'When I arrived home, bleeding, all my nails ripped off, completely wild, I was longing for Anna to warm salt water for me and bathe my wounds. But she couldn't help me. In fact, it was she who needed my help. She was in labour, and with no money, there was no chance of us getting any medical help for her. So I just had to get on with it. I encouraged her, helped her, and finally pulled my own son out. My first son. Then we had all this string, the umbilical cord, hanging around, and I didn't have any idea what to do with it, so I dashed into the kitchen, and brought back a knife. It wasn't even clean! I thought, "God, you've given me this boy, and you can either take him, or leave him. By leaving him, I would feel that my torture and everything that I've been through will remain as a testimony to my faith. I have come in a complete circle – beaten in jail, battered, bleeding, and left for dead – and here I am, with a sign of new life. Can I have this boy?" So I took the knife, and with whatever I found there, a rope or whatever, I tied a knot around the umbilical cord, and cut it. I looked down at my new son in my arms, and thanked God for him. We called him Kilele. In Swahili it means "Son of Trouble". And he was certainly born in trouble . . .

'But our troubles were not over. The authorities heard that I was not dead, as they thought, and they were hunting for me. I knew I had to leave. My future was so bleak in Sudan, dark and without hope. I believe that life is a struggle, but you need hope, a promise of better things in the future to make the struggle worthwhile. In my heart, I believed that some day I would be somebody, but at that time, I could see nothing but fear and danger. Anna was wonderful. She understood exactly how I felt. She knew that as long as I left, they would leave her alone. It was only me that they wanted, and we had no doubt that they would take me and slaughter me. They have slaughtered so many people in the name of Allah, because they believe that Allah wants them to kill infidels, and to kill and to be killed for Allah is the purest joy. Anna went and brought me all the money she had in this world, which amounted to about one pound, all our savings. I put it in a plastic carrier bag along with George Orwell's *Animal Farm*, and set off in nothing more than the shoes, trousers and T-shirt I was standing in. It was so painful to leave Anna. We would meet again. I knew we would meet again. I would go and prepare a home for her and "The Son of Trouble". If I survived, I would make sure they were both happy. More than anything else, however much of a struggle our lives turned out to be, they deserved some happiness. I remember how she told me that she loved me, and gave me her blessings. From that moment on, she and Kilele were my driving force. Knowing that I had people behind me who loved and needed me, that changed the shape of my life. It deepened my faith to think that someone like me, who is not a midwife, can deliver their own son, cut the umbilical cord, and the boy can survive – that is surely a miracle.'

Andrew was desperate to get out of Sudan. A train journey across the Sahara towards Egypt was the obvious answer, but he had no money for a ticket, and the voyage took five days and nights as it headed away from the northern part of Sudan. In the end, he boarded anyway, along with several other stowaways – not in, but on top of the carriage. For five days they perched in the scorching sunshine, with no food or water. And the train didn't go all the way. At the border at Wade Halpha, passengers had to get a ferry to continue their journey to Aswan in Egypt, before connecting with another train to Cairo.

'But again,' recalls Andrew, 'God works in mysterious ways. I happened to meet a student on that train who was going back to Egypt. We became good friends, and in the end, he offered to buy me a ticket right through to Cairo. That was the beginning of my new life. One of the first places that I was sent to was the Anglican Church, All Saints, in Cairo. Even though I was a Catholic, I was told that if I needed help, that was the place to go, where many Southern Sudanese were being given support. They were wonderful. They cleaned me up and told me to go to their stores and take any clothes and shoes I found there which fitted me. They fed me, and helped me find somewhere to live. They took care of me until I was able to start working. It was there that I met an Englishman called Andy Wheeler, who has since become the Adviser on the Sudanese Christian Church for the Archbishop of Canterbury. For the very first time, I was hit by the impact of meeting someone who really cared. I had never experienced that before – to come across someone who would listen and advise, somebody who was there for me when I really needed help. I needed food for my soul and my brain as well as my body. He opened doors, especially to education. He told me the Church would pay for me to do a course on oxyacetylene welding at the Italian Institute, Don Bosco, which would give me the practical skills of a trade. He said, "Andrew, you can put this on, wear this, come here and eat" – and I couldn't believe, coming from a Catholic background, that I was being shown such loving care by a Protestant. That was when I started to realize that the horizons of true Christianity are broad and infinite. We are one body. Day by day we sit and break bread together as a symbol of Jesus' body. His blood we drink. That realization changed me in so many ways. I became a Christian. Not a Catholic, not an Anglican. I will celebrate with you anywhere. If you want we can pray, in this room we can pray. Whatever your background or denomination, we are one in Christ.

'Eventually I managed to find work as a house boy, working in five different homes in order to get enough money to keep myself. I was always in touch with Anna, and I loved getting letters from her. Sometimes I was able to send back little gifts for her and Kilele with some of the many Sudanese students who were studying in Egypt. When they finished their exams, or went back for holidays, they would take presents and messages to her for me.

'One day when I'd been in Egypt for about seven months, I happened to bump into another Englishman who changed my life. He was middle-aged, and wandering around looking very lost. At first I didn't trust him, because a lot of people who come from Europe are drug dealers. Then I noticed how vulnerable he was, especially as the Egyptians can be quite dishonest and like parasites if they see a stranger who has money. I eventually went up and introduced myself. He told me his name was Tim Biles, and that although he wasn't wearing a dog collar, he was in fact an English minister sent by the bishop of his diocese in Salisbury to find out about the plight of Christians in Sudan. For a long time his diocese had been in contact with the Sudanese Christians, but communication had been broken because of the civil war. Tim was on a fact-finding mission.

'My English was very poor at that time, apart from the little I had learned at school, but I made him understand how dangerous it would be for him to go into the Sudan. Instead, I offered to take him from place to place in Cairo, introducing him to members of the displaced Sudanese community, all now refugees. Finally, I took him to the Ethiopian Embassy to get a visa, so that he could travel through Ethiopia rather than go through Khartoum. I could tell that a trust was growing between us. He kept wanting to do things for me – buy me food, for example – and I would say no because I had money of my own. It wasn't much, but I was not a beggar, and I needed him to understand that I wanted him to tell the world about the situation facing Christians in the Sudan. Then he asked me if I needed a watch because he wanted to buy me one. I said no, because why would I need a watch? You English need watches because you rush about, and you don't have time. I don't have a watch, but I have all the time in the world.

'Eventually, Tim went off on his journey through Ethiopia, where he came across a camp where there were about sixteen thousand really young, orphaned Southern Sudanese children. The eldest were only about seven years old, and yet they had walked all the way to Ethiopia, and then had to walk back again. They were just the victims of politics. Anyway, Tim was really shocked and moved when he met them. Then he went to Kenya, and from there up to my home town of Torit. It was there that he was the first outsider to witness the birth of the new Sudan Council of Churches. In the end, he took a letter back to England from the Catholic and the Anglican bishops, who were the only two people working there because of the civil war.

'When he got back to Cairo after about a month, he told me that he planned to write a book, because people in England needed to understand the plight of Christians in Southern Sudan. And then he said something which completely took my breath away. "I am going to take you to England."

'I was really melted, so happy. He realized I had no future where I was, that my life was in danger if I tried to go back home to Sudan. I said to him that if he really was going to take me to England, I had to know first of all what I would be doing there, because I had heard of people who had left the Sudan, and then were not allowed to go back. My son, Kilele, was about nine months old by then, and I knew I eventually wanted to be with him and Anna.

'After a great deal of thought and discussion, I made up my mind that this offer to go to England was too good to turn down.

Perhaps it was a dream come true, an opportunity to study properly, work hard, and get a good education at last.

'Tim had persuaded the Diocese of Salisbury to sponsor me, and I finally had a proper seat in an aeroplane – not just a shape in the sky half a mile above me, not travelling in a bag of coffee beans, but a seat which was paid for, and had my name on it.

'England was such a change for me – the culture, the weather, the language. It took me a while to acclimatize and adjust myself to this very new way of life. For three months I stayed with Tim and his family in Beaminster. I found it a bit difficult to adjust to the local community there because it was a retirement area, where many of the residents are quite elderly. All the younger ones took off every day to the big cities, or whatever. I found this so different from Sudanese culture, because where I had been brought up, the older you are, the wiser they consider you to be. At the centre of every family, you'll find an elder sitting by the fire telling stories, with all the children gathered around them. We didn't have to write down or read these stories from books, because they were just handed down to us. So when I came to Dorset, I felt very sorry for the elderly people I met through church, because they were all alone in their houses and cottages. I decided that I would break the pattern, and I kept going from one house to another, and saying things like, "Hello, Elizabeth, how are you?" They'd be really surprised to see me, and I'd invite myself in for a cup of tea. They probably only expected me to stay for five minutes, but often an hour later we'd still be sitting there, and I know they enjoyed my visits. My friend, Elizabeth even knitted me a woolly jumper. It was lovely, and I remember asking her how long it had taken her. She said it didn't matter what time it took, because the days were too long for her. Yes, the people of Salisbury diocese were so generous, really wonderful.

'After three months, they arranged for me to enrol at Weymouth

College, even though my English was still very broken with limited vocabulary. They offered me a place for two years to study for a B-Tech in Media Studies. It was so difficult for me. My first tutor was Scottish, and I just couldn't understand his accent. But I just worked and worked. Sometimes I would go to bed at three o'clock in the morning because I had an assignment to finish. Even the notes I took during lectures were hard for me, because I would write them down in Arabic, then check them again by translating them into English. But the ordeal of it all paid off. In the end, I not only passed my exams, but I was chosen as the Best Student of the Year. Lord Digby handed me a prize and certificate, and for the very first time in my life, I cried. I never cry. If somebody dies, I don't cry. Through all the torture and trauma, I didn't cry. But at that moment, I just couldn't help myself. I cried tears of relief and sheer happiness. I had achieved more than I could ever have dreamed of. I just wished that my grandmother could have been there to see me, and Anna and "Son of Trouble", so that they could witness that beautiful, fantastic occasion.

'In the two years since I had seen Anna, things had become very dangerous for her. The authorities had learned that I was in England, and they knew that I sometimes telephoned her. They were afraid that my wife might tell me secrets about what was happening in the Sudan, and that the West would come to hear things they would prefer to be kept quiet. They were hoping I would come back to the Sudan to find Anna, so that they could arrest and slaughter me. I knew that Anna and Kilele desperately needed to leave the country for their own safety.

'It was the Archbishop of Canterbury who came to our aid. He knew of my presence in Dorset, and he said that he would support my application if I applied for political asylum. It took several months, but it finally came through – I was granted permission to stay in England for four years. From then on, the Archbishop, the

Bishop of Salisbury and Tim Biles decided that they would work out a way to bring Anna and Kilele to England. In the end, Tim went and collected them himself. There was so much corruption in the Sudan at that time, and it was a matter of who you knew, and how much money you had to buy what you wanted, but he did it. So one day, three years after the last time I had seen my baby son, I found myself waiting at Heathrow Airport to welcome my wife and child. I waited and waited and waited. The plane landed, the passengers all came through, and there was no sign of them. All the long days, months and years since I had seen them – and yet those three hours were the hardest of all. But then, I saw them! I was shocked at how skinny Anna was, and she looked small and frightened, but oh, what a blessing to see her! I was overjoyed. Of course, Kilele didn't know me, even though he was holding a photo of me which he had been told was a picture of his father. It must have been overwhelming for him, but it was so fantastic to see them both!

'I know that it was very difficult for Anna, coming from a country where she had been fearful and hungry, to arrive in a comfortable, middle-class corner of Dorset. And her husband was a man she hardly knew. We had met when she was fourteen, and we hadn't been together long before I had left her alone, with a baby to bring up on her own. I don't know how she managed, especially as she assumed I would behave like a typical African man, expecting her to do everything for him. Instead, I was cooking and looking after myself, so she was very surprised. I remember saying to her, look, this is England. My mother is not here. Your mother is not here. We have no one but ourselves. We have to look to each other, work together, if we are going to make a go of things here. In the years since, I have come to realize that she is a wonderful mum, and if you talk about love, her heart is the place to find it. We've been through so much, but she is a truly wonderful woman. We decided eventually that we would like a proper recognition of our marriage. The Bishop of Salisbury, who had worked so hard for our reunion, came and blessed us. It was very special. In time, our family expanded. Kilele is ten years old, and our next son we named Timothy, after our dear friend, Tim Biles. Timothy is now six years old, and Tim Biles and his wife are his godmother and father.

'I find it hard to reconcile my upbringing as a Christian in the Sudan with what I see here in England. When I was a child, we had to walk six or seven miles to go to church to sing God's praises, and I always felt, yes, I was giving my soul to God, and He was taking care of me. But here there is a very comfortable life, a consumer society, where not many young people go to church. That's because people here have so much, they've become lazy, and don't care about the things that really matter. Why should people go to church when they can watch Pam on 'Songs of Praise' bringing Christianity right into their homes? In my country, we were tortured and persecuted for our faith. We had to deny what we believed in order to get food and work. And yet in this country, for instance in Ireland, you Christians are eating each other, just as big fish eat the smaller ones. Christians fight themselves, kill their brothers, their own fellow Christians. I find that very difficult to comprehend.

'To me, my faith is a continuing process. I keep discovering more about what I believe all the time. And it happens when I am alone, just as I was in the bush as a child. There is so much more to life than I ever understood then. And because I have now qualified as a cameraman and journalist, my people have high expectations of me. They need me to tell the world what is going on in the Sudan. I have a responsibility to give a voice to the voiceless. I can speak – not criticize, but at least try to amend the wrongs, publicize the injustices by letting people around the world know what is happening.

'I go back to my country regularly now, but only to the rebel controlled area, because my life would be in danger if I went anywhere near Khartoum. But even if I am protected by the rebels, I am not protected from shells or anti-personnel weapons. I hear explosions all around me, and look back to see someone behind me is gone, and I just pray to be allowed to continue. My prayer now is the same as it was all those years ago. "Lord, use me as an ambassador, let me do your work to the maximum. And if one day, you have no further use for me, then I don't want to die a painful death, losing my limbs, or dying slowly in the hands of the enemy. Once they capture you, they will just cut you slowly, slowly, until you die. I pray that will not happen. If the worst comes to the worst, just give me one bullet in my head, and let me die quickly." And the moment I start praying, I feel strong and powerful. Honestly, when I am in the war zone, I don't have time to drop to my knees and pray. I just talk. I talk to God, and I know He hears me. I mean, if I just read from a book of prayer, that would be somebody else's words. So I just talk, because God listens. He knows my heart, and hears my prayer.

'I have been through so much. I was deprived of the essential things any child in this world deserves. I saw my own niece blown up in front of me, simply because she wanted a drink of water. I've been shot at, starved, tortured and beaten to a pulp all because I would not renounce my faith. On the night I nearly died, I brought forth life as I acted as midwife for my own son. I have been a refugee with no home and no prospects – when all I had left was my faith, my pride, and my never-ending hope that God would bring me through. And one day, I pray that I can go home with my head held high – free to enjoy all the privileges of being treated as an equal to everyone else. And most of all, free to practise my faith, to praise my God. I will fight for what I believe until the end of my life.

'And perhaps one day I will take my sons back to the bush

where I sat with the sheep for hours each day, and tell them about that small boy wearing no clothes, watching planes going overhead, and dreaming of a very different future.

'Their future. Without fear. And with the dignity and hope that every living human being deserves. Please God.'

Rod

Anyone who can think back to 1976, will remember that advert — the group of tanned, obviously popular James Bond lookalikes all winging their effortless way through clear blue skies beneath colourful hang-gliders, before landing without as much as a bump to find beautiful girls waiting for them with ice-cold Martinis in their hands, and meaningful smiles on their lips. It was enough to make any young man green with envy — and Rod Surrage was no exception. As a married man with two very small daughters, the beautiful girls were appealing, but out of bounds — but the hang-gliding? Well, as Rod and Adrian, his colleague at Eastern Carpet Stores, watched the advert, the sight of those hang-gliders, and the thought of being able to fly unaided through the sky, stirred something akin to passion within them. They *had* to try it. The next thing they knew, they'd booked a course, and found themselves lined up with a handful of other enthusiasts (none of them looking remotely like James Bond, any more than Rod and Adrian did!) ready to take their first running leap off Devil's Dyke. They took to the sky on a two-seater kite with their instructor, and after a perfect landing, they were hooked. With just an hour or two in the classroom, and a rudimentary knowledge of aerodynamics and wind movement behind him, Rod stood at the edge of that almost sheer drop, feeling not fear, but an adrenalin rush of anticipation.

The following week, wearing a special helmet which contained a receiver allowing him to hear the instructor's comments in his ear, he was aware that he was very much on his own. But then that was what had drawn him to hang-gliding in the first place – the thought that as he left the ground, all he had to keep him from plummeting into the side of the hill was the kite above him, and his own reactions to the elements. The freedom, the silence, the view, the peace, the wind on his face, the lift of his spirits as he soared like a bird in the sky – that was hang-gliding for Rod: an instant fascination which became a compulsion.

Rod and Adrian first flew without an instructor on the nursery hill of Stevning Bowl, and on his first solo flight, Adrian fractured his ankle as he landed. 'Perhaps that should have been a warning to me,' says Rod now. But it wasn't. Adrian hobbled around on a walking stick for weeks after that. He even voiced his doubts about the wisdom of hang-gliding to Rod, but it made no difference to either of them. Both men went out and bought second-hand kites, and were flinging themselves off hilltops again as soon as they possibly could.

In the mid-seventies, hang-gliding was a new sport to this country, and the kites were very basic. Rigallo initially designed the first hang-glider as a directional parachute for space craft re-entry. Once sportsmen discovered its potential for pure pleasure, they found, like Rod, that 'if you run like hell, you literally float all the way down to the bottom of the hill. As long as you can hear a flapping noise from the sail at the back of you, you know you are going fast enough. If the noise stops, then you're in trouble – the kite stalls, falls out of the sky, and you hit the hill hard.' Accidents like Adrian's and much worse, happened often but were hushed up. Tales abounded of injuries where other glider pilots climbed down the side of the hill to remove the hang-glider before they called for help, so that the sport would not be brought into disrepute. When the paramedics eventually arrived, an explanation that the fall happened during a rock climbing expedition was likely to be accepted without question.

As new generations of kite came into use, each one was more technical than the last – more efficient, less steady and therefore more dangerous. The early kites were slower and more forgiving. Those later models left no margin for error. You had to know how to fly them. After three years of flying, Rod had progressed from his first generation kite, which was basically a big diamond with poles threaded through it, to the second generation when he bought a new 'Falcon III'. Flushed with confidence and enthusiasm, he skipped a grade and went straight on to the Chargus Cyclone, which was little more than a flying wing, six foot long from front to back with a thirty-six foot wingspan. Being only eleven stone, Rod was the lightest possible weight for the larger size of Cyclone – so when he took off on it, it certainly flew! He remembers being at the top of the 'stack' on it. Even the new prototype being tested that day couldn't get high enough to reach him.

'And that efficiency,' recalls Rod now, 'was my downfall. With the older kites, once you'd put an input into them to turn left, you'd know you could almost have a cigarette while you waited for it to get round to turning. But with the later generation of kites, you only had to move a little, and they responded. My trouble was that, because I'd missed a generation, I assumed that I could fly the Cyclone as I had flown kites in the past. By the time I found out that I couldn't, it was all too late . . .'

On any Sunday morning, he would be up at six o'clock ringing the Met Office to find out the direction and speed of the wind that day. If it was north, or north-easterly, then he was in the car by seven o'clock heading down to Devil's Dyke. A west wind would have him speeding along to the other end of the Downs near Shoreham. If easterly, he would set off on a hundred-mile journey to Castle Morton near Tewkesbury.

'You never flew alone,' he says, 'because you had no idea what might happen. So once you'd got to the hill, you would just sit there and wait for someone else to turn up. As long as you had company, you knew you could start flying. I just couldn't stand that waiting period, as flying was such a fantastic feeling. I knew people had accidents, and I always said that if I broke something, I would stop flying. I know now that I was lying. Even if I'd broken a leg or an arm, I would still have gone straight back up again as soon as I was able.'

Although Rod's Malaysian-born wife, Natalie, and his two daughters, Shirley and Michelle, sometimes came with him on his hang-gliding trips, mostly his compulsion with the hobby excluded them. 'I remember once when we had quite a serious break-up for about six weeks or so, I went back to apologize and tell Natalie I loved her. I sat on the settee and said, "Look, I'll do anything you ask, but please don't ask me to give up hang-gliding!" It was like a drug. I had to have my fix.'

Melanie and the children happened to be with him on 24 September 1979 when Rod arrived at Devil's Dyke for his third flight on the Cyclone. 'Looking back, it all happened so suddenly. I was obviously flying too slowly, as I had on the previous kites. I was travelling parallel with the hill when the kite stalled, and its nose went down, turning downwind towards the hill. In a desperate attempt to keep it flying, I increased the speed, which is the one thing you are told never to do. I remember thinking, "Uh-oh, I've really messed things up here," and worrying about my family because if I had an accident, how would the children and Natalie get home, as she didn't have a driving licence at the time. Then I switched into automatic safety mode, thinking quickly about what I could do to save myself. Where should I head? Perhaps I could just fly into the car park and land between the cars? I'm not going to hit that Rolls-Royce though, I remember thinking, I might have a million pounds in insurance through the British Hang-Gliding Association, but no, I don't think I fancy hitting that! All in all, I probably had about five seconds as I lost height after I stalled, time for many thoughts to go through my mind. Most of all, I remember thinking, Well, if you break your leg, tough!

'As the kite was still turning to the right, I decided to turn right in a "wing-over", where you almost stand the kite on end, and fly round one wing. In the process of that I felt my harness pull tight as the kite responded. At first, I felt relief – then *crunch*! The wing-tip must have touched the ground, and dragged me down. I was told much later that I had only needed another five or six foot to have cleared the hill completely.

'On impact, I was holding the control bar with my arms outstretched, so that as the kite hit the ground, I quickly followed! To make matters worse, I was lying face down in my prone harness, which meant that I swung through the control bar hitting the keel boom with my head. The elbow of my outstretched right arm was dislocated, and my crash helmet split in two as my neck took the brunt of the impact.

'I can remember very clearly the kite hitting the ground. Next thing, all was silent as I lay there. My glasses were digging into my nose, and I shouted to another pilot to come and take them off because they hurt. That pilot had been taught enough to know that after an accident you should never move the victim, which had me swearing at him until in the end he did remove them. It was later that I realized that the pain of those glasses had probably been keeping me conscious. The next thing I knew, the paramedics were there, the kite had gone, I was wearing a neck collar and was being rolled over on to a metal spinal stretcher.

'Natalie spoke to me in the ambulance, having made sure that the children were being taken care of. Although they hadn't seen the accident, she had, and she was obviously very shaken. I remember her telling me that everything would be all right. Then she left, the doors closed, and we started moving. Perhaps I might have believed what she'd said about it all being all right then, because thankfully I was in no pain, but that in itself was a frightening thought. If there was no pain, how severe was the fracture . . . ?

'The attendant kept asking me my name, how old I was, and my address, and then he asked again — how old are you, Rod? Where do you live? Over and over — and I knew why he was doing that because I used to be in the St John Ambulance. I said, "I know what you're doing. You're trying to establish my level of conscious- ness . . ." And the next time I opened my eyes, the ambulance was backing into the Accident and Emergency entrance of Cuckfield Hospital.

'I now know that I was only at Cuckfield for a few hours, before they realized the seriousness of my injury required the kind of specialist treatment I would be able to get at the Royal Infirmary Hospital in Cardiff. The ironic thing, looking back, is that the first powered flight I ever had was in the emergency helicopter which took me there — an old Air Sea Rescue Wessex. At any other time, I would have loved every second of that flight!'

Immediately he arrived at Cardiff, Rod was wheeled in for surgery to remove bone chips from his neck. For three weeks he was in intensive care, for some of the time on a life support system which had to do his breathing for him. If he looked at the team nursing him to see if he could get a clue as to the severity of his injury, they were only ever totally professional. Whenever they moved him, it required no less than four nurses, one to hold his head, one each side, and one at his feet so that he was always turned in a straight line to ensure that the fracture was never stressed. He had sandbags up each side of his head, and ten pounds of traction screwed into his skull and hanging over the end of the bed to keep his neck stretched.

'I remember lying on my back feeling as if my arms and legs were pointing up into air when I could see that they weren't, and that gave me a pretty good idea of how bad my condition was. My brain was obviously remembering the position of my limbs when I hit the keel boom and broke my neck. It took months and months for me to lose that impression in my brain. I used to lie in bed and tell myself I was lying flat, that my legs were not up in the air. It was the first real indication to me that my injury was very severe.'

Eventually, while Rod was still in intensive care, the doctor came to take his ventilator out. 'I remember him asking me, "Do you know what's happened to you?" I said, "Yes, I've broken my neck." He then said, "You've compacted and shattered vertebrae three, four and five – and I want you to accept the fact that you'll never move again." Just like that.

'I looked at him, and said, "No way. I can only accept the fact that I *might* never move again." Perhaps I was still living in cuckoo land then, but I had to believe I would get better. I had to hang on to that hope.'

Rod spent five weeks in all at the Cardiff Royal Infirmary, three weeks in intensive care, and two weeks on the trauma ward. Then he was moved to the Rookwood Spinal Injuries Unit at Llandaff, an area of Cardiff, where he spent the next nine months recovering from an operation to graft a bone from his hip to his neck, and wire all the vertebrae into place to give his neck support. As a result, down the back of his neck where his scar now is, there are no vertebrae lumps, just smooth skin. It's impossible for him to turn his head completely from side to side. 'Most people can look over their shoulders,' he says, 'I can't.' While Rod was at Rookwood, it took three months of lying flat on his back in bed before the bones healed. 'I had what they call Passive Movement Physiotherapy, where they bend your knees, hips and arms, and rotate your feet and hands. Then, once my neck was more stable, they began swinging my legs from side to side, hoping to keep me supple in case there was any chance of recovery. One day when I was in the spinal unit, I was very chuffed when I thought I could move a bicep. They crowded round to watch me, and said, "Go on then!" And I couldn't. It just wouldn't move. They could see how gutted I was, and they tried telling me not to worry – perhaps it might move, perhaps it wouldn't. That was a bleak moment for me though.

'I often used to wonder, as everyone in that situation does, *why me?* But then I would look across to the guy in the next bed who was able to move his upper body a bit because his break was not as severe as mine. He had internal complications though, which are much harder to deal with, and I began to feel quite fortunate that I wasn't suffering in the same way. I just thought how lucky I was not to have been disfigured or brain-damaged, considering how hard my head hit that hill. It could have been so much worse.'

Not many people could look at Rod today, twenty-two years on, paralysed from the neck down, and think of him as 'lucky'. On the other hand, I have rarely met someone with a more practical, down-to-earth attitude than this man who aspired to so much, but is now physically able to do so little. There is no element of self-pity, only a solid determination to get on with life, whatever the limitations. His sense of humour helps. He laughs a lot, not least at himself. He's great company, enjoying conversations that come to him mainly through the telephone (which he operates pneumatically by sucking a tube with his mouth), as a radio ham, and more recently through the internet, on the computer which he operates with a mouth stick.

He certainly doesn't give the impression of being lonely,

although loneliness overwhelmed him a few months after his accident when his social worker in hospital asked to see him privately. Once the door was shut, she sat on the front of her desk and told him that she had bad news for him. That news was that Natalie had decided that she didn't want him to come home again. From her point of view, their marriage was at an end. 'I think that was probably the time I felt lowest of all. It was hard to accept — especially as Natalie was a trained nurse, and knew that while I was so ill, one of the things I treasured most was the fact that she was by my side. Until that moment, in spite of all that had happened, I felt that at least I hadn't lost everything — but suddenly she too was gone.

'In May 1980, I was moved to Holy Cross Hospital in Haslemere, which was much nearer to home. Natalie brought the children in to see me regularly, but then would usually drive off, or sit in the car. Very occasionally she might come in to collect them. I remember asking her one day if I hadn't had my accident, would we still be together? She didn't even look at me, but carried on staring out of the window as she replied, "I doubt it." I think in her mind, our marriage was over even before the accident. My condition just gave her a reason to go.

'One day, Shirley, who was probably about eight at that time, started talking about "When you get well, Daddy" — and I had to say, "Darling, you know, Daddy's not ill. I just can't move." Then I went on to explain to her exactly what had happened, because it seemed the right time to tell her everything. "And Mummy and Daddy love you both very much, but we can't live together any more, so Daddy won't be coming home." Shirley looked at Natalie, and it was almost as if a penny had dropped. Then she looked back at me, and said, "Oh, I see."' After Rod moved to his present home near Guildford, visits by his daughters became more rare, and finally he didn't see either of them for years until a few weeks before Shirley's eighteenth birthday. However, now they are grown-up, Rod is in constant contact with both Shirley and Michelle.

Romance didn't abandon Rod completely once Natalie was gone. Just over a year after his accident, when he was still in his early thirties, he was spotted by a seventeen-year-old auxiliary nurse called Gill. Much later, he was to learn that the moment she saw him, she decided that he was the man with whom she wanted to spend the rest of her life. The rapport between them was instant, and when Rod left Holy Cross two years later, Gill went with him. They finally married in 1984, although Rod says that during the months leading up to their wedding, they fought like cat and dog. 'How she ever stayed with me, I don't know, but in spite of the rows, we were very telepathic in a way. I'd think, oh Gill, I just fancy a bottle of wine, and she'd come in twenty minutes later carrying a bottle, thinking that she would surprise me!'

Their life together was never easy, because before they got married Gill developed multiple sclerosis, and later needed help with everyday life just as much as he did. They had to rely on carers who came in to provide practical support for them both. That made Rod feel doubly helpless, especially when Gill was poorly. 'It was so frustrating for me to know that she needed to go to the toilet, or that she'd like a cup of tea, and I simply couldn't help her – or myself.'

In time, Gill became desperate to have a child of their own, but because of her MS, the chances were that she would end up in a wheelchair. Rod wasn't prepared to bring a child into the world with one parent who couldn't do anything, and another who was going to be very limited. Then, in January 1990, Gill told him she was going out to see someone, and an hour later Rod found out that she had packed her bags and her suitcases had gone. 'Although that wasn't the last I saw of her, it was the last time she stayed here.'

Rod was alone again. He missed Gill's love and companionship very deeply. "We were a formidable team, and people said that once we'd got our hearts set on something, then everyone knew they were up against a gang. Since then, I've been on my own, and felt very lost for a long time. I had to take control of my own life again, because Gill had always made sure things were done for me. I've had to become more self-dependent – and that's probably good. Fortunately, one step I had already taken in 1987 was to start to organize the care I needed throughout the day. Of course, I've had some really terrific carers, whose company I very much value. But I suppose, if people are here in the flat because they are working for money, you never know whether they're really friends, or just doing a job. I need their help so much though, and I've always been very careful to choose people with personalities I enjoy having around.

'Sometimes I'll say to my carers, "I don't want to play this game any more. I need to get up. I just want to go for a walk." I'll have five minutes of feeling sorry for myself, then that's it. It might not happen again for another six months. I'd be lying if I said that suicide has never crossed my mind. Whenever it does, I simply think about it as a piece of information. I know how to do it by myself, without any help. If I didn't want to be here, I wouldn't be, but it's the thought of how it would hurt my daughters that always stops me.'

Today, he still feels no pain, except for a bit of discomfort in his neck because he does everything with it, such as using his computer or typing 'hunt and peck' with a mouth stick. 'When I've been on the computer for maybe six or seven hours, that's a lot of neck movement, and I've got an 18 or 19 inch neck now. I've always had a thick neck, but there's no truth in the rumour that it holds up a thick head!'

Those biceps in which he had sensed movement quite early on are now reasonably mobile, but because the triceps behind are dead, their movement is not very helpful. 'You learn a lot about your body by what you can and can't do,' he says. 'If I could bend my arm, I wouldn't be able to straighten it up again because there are no triceps. But if I'm sitting up in my wheelchair now, I can lift my elbows out to the side. I have a certain amount of movement in my shoulders, although none in my hands. I can throw myself round the chair a bit to get comfortable in a very haphazard sort of way.

'Over the years, I've learned to value what I have, and to understand what my body is trying to say to me. I've learned that just because you can't feel the skin, it doesn't mean that you can't feel inside. As I lay here, at one time I would not have been able to feel my shoulders or my back. I can now. But if you sit me up, you could stick a pin in my shoulders and back, and I wouldn't feel it, even though I can feel the pressure of the pin. Whether it's psychosomatic, I don't know, but if that sense was taken away from me, then I would feel the loss.

'There are other losses I feel keenly. I miss hugs. I miss sunshine. I miss being treated as I was when I was able-bodied — like, for example, the typical incident when I was sitting with some friends round a table in a club, and a guy had been talking to me for half an hour or so, asking me all about my accident, then he stood up and said to my friend sitting next to me, "Would he like another pint?" He didn't ask me direct. It's the "Does he take sugar?" syndrome. In spite of all the work they've done over the last twenty years to try and bring disability into the open a bit more, you still get people like him who insist on talking to the carer as if the person in the wheelchair is not there.

'And there are other things that still hit me hard even now. I hate not being able to call the nurse in hospital with the buzzer, not being able to give myself a drink, and worst of all, not being able to feed myself. When I go out to a restaurant, I loathe the fact that I have to be fed. If something gets dripped down the front of me, I am so self-conscious. I use an external catheter, so that's OK — except when it comes off and you're sitting in the middle of a supermarket, and a big dark patch suddenly appears around my front. I just make a beeline for the door — and home. But the indignity of all still gets to me twenty years on.'

Rod has wondered how he would feel if a miracle cure for his condition were suddenly announced. 'Apprehensive probably, in that I would want to be sure of very good odds that I would end up better than I am now. My dread about any operation is that it would take away the little mobility I already have.

'A friend of mine said something the other week that I've thought about a lot since. She said that I must have agreed to this before I was born. It seemed such an odd thing to say, but I do think we are all on earth to learn something — and perhaps I was lacking. I just don't know. People say you've got past and future lives. There are many different theories as to what or who God is — whether He's a physical or a spiritual being. I don't believe in the conventional image of God, but I do believe that we all have an inner strength, a sense of self worth, that we can call upon in times of need. I do lie here and pray to God when things seem to be going wrong. I just pour out my heart and go to sleep. What's strange is how often the very next day, things start going right again. Is that because I've got a different outlook the following day? Is there a vast hand at work? There have been times when I've not been exactly frightened, but certainly anxious. Take the evening in January that Gill actually left. She went at six o'clock, and because the heating was up a bit high, I was starting to get hot and dry-mouthed. Worse still, I looked down to see that my drainage bag was full as well. I glanced at the clock, and it was seven. I knew Gill had phoned a carer to come in, but he wouldn't be arriving until half past nine. Who could possibly help me? I found myself thinking about my old friend, Bob, whom I'd not seen for ages, wishing that he might think it's time to pay me a call. A quarter of an hour later, Bob arrived! I was so pleased to see him, and told him he was the answer to a prayer. He told me that he had come in from work, had some dinner, fallen asleep in the chair, then at seven o'clock woken up with a start thinking that he must come and see me.

'When I look back on the accident now, I'm relieved that it was my fault. I stalled and crashed. It was pilot error, so I have only myself to blame. I don't know how I'd feel if I was lying here thinking badly about someone else who had hit me with a car, and ruined my life. I am able to forgive myself, so feel no bitterness about what happened. But I am also aware that if I had known that day what I know now, nothing much would have changed. I may not have gone flying that day, but it would probably have been the next day, or the day after that. I loved flying that much. I think that picture of hang-gliders on the wall over there says it all. "The more you put into living, the more you get out of life." I believe that. This may not have turned out to be the life I envisaged, but it's the life I've got — and it's a pretty good life too. I get down the pub every now and then. I go out to restaurants. I go on holiday to find the sunshine. Things could be a great deal worse.

'Over the last year or so, I've been writing a lot of poetry about love and feelings. One poem I wrote recalled when I was at school, coming back on a boat from Ostend. As the white cliffs of Dover became visible through the fog, my eyes filled with tears at the thought of how wartime servicemen must have felt to come back and see the shape of home in those cliffs. All these years later, that memory moved me so much, I found myself crying again, so I simply had to put my feelings into poetry. I don't bother now to hide how I feel. If I want to, I just cry my heart out. Why shouldn't I?

'And even now, all these years later, I still look out the window

Eileen

Twenty-five years ago, Eileen Harrild and her chartered surveyor husband, Tony, found themselves a lovely house in an up-and-coming commuter town not far from Glasgow and Edinburgh. It was the perfect place to bring up children, with friendly neighbours and excellent schools. Before long, their first son, Anthony, was born. Two years later, he was joined by his brother, Andrew. Next, came Jennifer, who was four years younger than Andrew. For Eileen, a daughter was a special pleasure, having grown up herself in a family where she was an only girl with six brothers! Then, as icing on the cake, Jack completed Eileen and Tony's quartet two years later.

Eileen always knew that while her children were young, she would want to be a full-time mum, and she looks back on those years when her life was devoted entirely to her own youngsters as very precious. But as Jack grew up and went to school himself, she started to think about the profession she had enjoyed so much before becoming a mother. She had trained as a Physical Education teacher, and had always loved the opportunity of passing on her own enthusiasm for the subject. She had taught secondary school children in the past, but the supply teaching post that came up when she resumed her career turned out to be with primary school pupils. The one and a half days she started working soon stretched to two and a half – before finally, she was asked to go for an interview for a full-time post which involved travelling around a number of schools in the area. What attracted her most was the fact that she would be based in her own local primary school just a mile away. As their commuter town expanded, so had its school, until by that time it was one of the biggest primary schools in the whole of Scotland, with six hundred pupils.

Eileen was delighted when she got the job. That was why on 13 March 1996, she was with an excited class of five years old at the start of their gym lesson.

And from that day on, the whole world remembers the name of Dunblane Primary School.

'If a group of five, six or seven year olds run into a gym, there's something amiss if they're not really keen to get started,' says Eileen. 'I've always loved to see the joy on their faces when you help them do something they think they can't manage. They can't wait to get home and tell their mums how clever they've been! Most of all, they're so honest. If you're under the weather, or you've changed your hair colour, they'll come up and remind you. I remember wearing a pair of Coca-Cola socks one day, and they couldn't keep their eyes off them! I don't think they heard a word I said to them, because they were so fascinated by my socks!

'We worked on different skills throughout the year. From August until December, they would practise their game skills, depending on the age group, so that the older ones would actually be playing netball, tennis, hockey or cricket. Then leading up to Christmas I would teach modern and Scottish dancing, which was always good fun. After Christmas until March, we did gymnastics all term, then during the summer term, we would be outside playing tennis or cricket, or working towards Athletic Awards. It was a busy schedule.

'My timetable was pretty relentless, teaching from nine till half past three every day non-stop – no breaks, except for a quick lunch. It could be very exhausting, but really enjoyable too. I worked on a fortnightly rota, so that every day I was at a different school. I was teaching over a thousand children, but actually saw each child in their school once a fortnight. Then, the week I wasn't there, their own teachers would follow up what I had covered with them in the lesson before.

'Because I met so many youngsters, it took a while to get to know all their names, but at Dunblane it was easier because I was local, and often some of the children would come up and say, "You taught my mummy or daddy," which made me feel pretty ancient! It was very sweet really, especially as I felt a special connection because through their parents, they knew me. The little ones would always be trying to tell me things, about their birthday perhaps, or something that seemed important to them, and you know how long it can take a five year old to tell you a story! Sometimes I had to hurry them on, or ask them nicely to tell me later, otherwise we'd never get going. And trust is always so important, especially when you're in charge of a class of perhaps thirty small children who are hardly used to being away from their mums. They had to get to know the language I use which could be different from what they had grown to expect from their own class teacher. They needed to get to know me, because I had to be sure how far I could let them go, bearing in mind that safety is always the number one priority. If I had an unruly class, I needed to tame them, rein them in before I could let them loose on beams, ropes or frames.

'Everyone develops at their own pace, and one of the challenges of being a good teacher is to try and meet every child's individual need. Sometimes when the class was very busy with tasks I had set them, I would take one or two children aside. I would never take one out on their own because, although these were youngsters who were struggling a bit, I didn't want them to feel they were being picked on. When they're only five, one of the first skills they learn in the gym is step patterns, like hopscotch, for instance, which is very difficult when they have to use their head to count, then co-ordinate their feet at the same time! Hopping on its own is quite a challenge, so is standing on one foot and balancing, and some youngsters find skipping very hard to master. I remember one little lad in my Dunblane class who had great trouble with skipping, and I spent ages with him, holding his hand as he stepped, then hopped, then put the other foot forward. Slowly, so slowly, we went over and over the movement, until I let go of his hand, and he was off, galloping round the gym like a kangaroo. He wasn't skipping, but he thought he was. It was lovely to see him!

'That week leading up to 13 March had been really strange. A number of things I remember especially. The first was that in the Holy Family Catholic church in Dunblane where I belong, we had a mission. Tony and I thought we would just pop along to show support on the first night, but in fact when we got there, the church was packed. Well, what a fantastic evening that was! It held us so much, and touched us all. It made us stop and think because it seemed relevant to our own lives. In the end the church was full for the whole week, and made a tremendous spiritual impact on me.

'But then, bearing in mind what a meaningful, thought-provoking week it was in our church, we found that when we were driving back after those evenings, the sky was amazing. It wasn't just normal clouds, but more like the aurora borealis. Absolutely breathtaking, and it was not only me who noticed it. Another friend rang me from St Andrew's one night, and mentioned how glorious the sky looked. In fact, it was even written about in the *Scotsman* newspaper, and noted by the Observatory as being most unusual.

'Then, on the Sunday before that week began, we had a family gathering which included my father, mother, my aunt and uncle. We hadn't all been together under one roof for such a long time. We had a lovely day with all of them joining our own family of six for dinner. It really was a fun day, and we even took a film of ourselves because we were enjoying each other's company so much. None of us knew just what lay ahead of us that week. I often look back and think that all those unusual occurrences during the days before the 13th were meant to be.

'Another lovely memory from the evening before the shooting was that Tony had been working late, so late that on his way back he stopped at a garage and bought me a bunch of flowers. This may not seem so unusual for some men, but Tony was never a "flower" man, and I can't recall him ever having done that before – certainly not after working late! Even odder was the fact that the farmer he had been seeing that evening had the same surname as the man I was going to meet so tragically the next day.

'Some time later our priest told us some unbelievable stories about how little things have happened to people which, with hindsight, they realize had special meaning. I'm not a superstitious person, but I wonder if we were being prepared mentally for what we were going to have to face.

'It began as a perfectly normal day, except that it was snowing which the youngsters were thrilled about. The infants had assembly between nine and nine thirty in the big school hall, so the class who were coming to join me in the gym straight after that were already changed. While I could hear their young voices singing in the hall next door, I had a lot to do that morning. I was putting out more big equipment than they had ever used before, and it took a bit of time to lay it all out properly. I remember going back to my room to collect my file, and left it open on the bench because I needed to keep an eye on what I was doing with each group. The children were divided up into groups with the names of colours or animals. If they were doing a topic on the zoo, then I would use animal names, such as the "Lion Group". That made it easier for them to know what they were supposed to be doing, and where they should start.

'As I heard the assembly finishing, I was being more vigilant than ever because there was a lot of big equipment out. The top third of the gym was covered with large pieces, but the bottom third was left empty until I'd got the class warmed up. The children knew the routine. Warm up, then they would help me put out the rest of the equipment. But because they had been sitting still for half an hour, they were anxious to get into the gym, and the first three ran in because they couldn't wait! Now, it's part of their learning process that they don't just run in and jump on anything they like, so I put on my stern face, and made them go back out and line up again. Along with the children came their class teacher, a lovely lady called Gwen. I'd known Gwen a long time, and she had been at the school for about ten years, so she was very popular. She was only going to be there for a few minutes before she had to leave, but the assistant head teacher was planning to come in and replace her once she'd left. Then Mary came and joined us too. She was a Special Duty Attendant with responsibility for one particular pupil in the class. Gwen went to sit on the bench at the back of the gym, and Mary sat behind her. I stopped the class to tell them what they were going to do – and that was when he came in.'

Even today, like many people in Dunblane, Eileen cannot bring herself to give 'that man' a name. In her mind, he is less than human, a non-entity, not important. As such, he is worthy of nothing. They have neither the interest nor the strength to think of his personality and problems with anything other than indifference.

'To get to us, he had to go through two sets of doors, walk past the changing rooms and my room, then come through two glass doors into the gym. I was at that end of the gym because I always had to have the whole class within my sight, but I was aware of movement as soon as the door started opening. It swung open – and I saw him. I watched him walk towards me, and saw he was in combat gear, armed with a variety of guns. His hand was stretched out towards me, and he didn't say a word. He just looked straight at me, and in that moment I knew he wasn't mad. He *meant* to kill me. He was simply bad, evil personified as he shot to kill. For the next four minutes, he was the devil incarnate. No doubt about it. My automatic reaction after that first shot was to put both arms up to protect myself – and that's when he shot me again – four times in all, through both forearms, another ricocheted straight through my hand, and one more hit me in the chest.

'Then he turned to see Gwen sitting close to me, near the door. She didn't even have time to get up before he shot her. She died immediately.

'Mary's life was probably saved by the fact that just before he came in, she had stood up to see the little boy in her charge. She was the next to be targeted, but thank God, although he shot her in the back of the head and legs, they weren't the fatal wounds they might have been.

'I remember seeing all the children scattered around the gym. It happened so quickly that I don't think they believed what they saw when the shooting started. I realized I had been shot because I was bleeding, but my head was saying this can't be happening! There was no pain, just fear – and disbelief. I didn't fall to my knees after I was shot, but stumbled over into the alcove where the equipment was kept, and just slumped on to the floor along with Mary and several children who had also been wounded. There was a child lying across me who had gunshot wounds on her legs.

'I can remember thinking, somebody help us – stop him, stop him somebody – but nobody could stop him. Then I heard the sound of the glass door being opened at the top of the gym, and I thought perhaps he was going away. But it soon became clear what he was going to do. He started to shoot into a class room. Fortunately, I learned later, the teacher there had been aware that something dreadful was going on, so she told the class to get down on the floor. He sprayed the whole classroom with bullets – there were even holes in the backs of some of the chairs – but fortunately the children were safe. By this time, he was on the patio area, when he took aim across the playground to where a teacher was taking her class along the corridor towards the library. The teacher was injured in the back of the head by a bullet which ricocheted off the glass, but because she had managed to get the children down on the floor, none of that group were hurt.

'It's true what people say that, when some senses go, others become very heightened. My sense of smell and hearing just took over, because I was aware that I needed to know where that man was – not that I could really have done anything. I remember being very aware of the smell of gun powder, cordite, and of fresh blood. A group of children, some injured, some dead, had huddled where they'd fallen in the middle of the hall. The children with Mary and me in the alcove were beginning to scream in pain and terror, and I hushed them urgently, warning them not to make a sound, so they became deathly silent. Then we heard him coming back into the gymn – and I thought, this is it! We're going to die! But he didn't come towards us. Instead he circled the group of youngsters lying in the middle of the hall, shooting at them again and again.

'Under the alcove, there was a huge pile of rubber mats that we used around the gym equipment, and I remember thinking that if I could pull the mats over us, we might be safe. If I could just get the children underneath the mats, he might not see us. But my hand, which had been shot through, was useless. I couldn't move my arms, I had no strength in them. Also, I was aware that I had been shot in my chest. The mats were so heavy, I simply couldn't budge them, and I was terrified that any movement would make him come back to us again. He did turn his attention to the alcove again, but only to spray bullets over the top of us.

'I think he was frightened of being caught at that moment, because the whole nightmare had been going on for about three minutes by then. A lot of people have asked me since, how did I know how long it was? Well, you have to remember that I was very used to timing people running distances, so you get quite familiar with time. But my mind was in total shock right then, with disbelief, fear and terror. I thought I was going to die. I was the teacher. I felt responsible for what was happening. This was *my* class. Why was he doing this? What could I do to stop it?

'Then, I think, he went to the top of the gym. By that time, a teacher had arrived with a student member of staff from the art room. I think the man must have seen them, and realized people were on their way — so he turned the gun on himself.

'But at the time, I didn't know any of that. All I remember was the terrible silence as we waited for him to start again. Nobody moved. Nobody cried. Nobody whimpered. Nothing. That silence seemed to go on for a very long time, and then people started to react to their wounds, crying, screaming, moaning. I started saying to Mary that I'd been shot in the chest, and she was bleeding as I'd never seen in my life from the back of her head and legs. The least injured children were beginning to stand up, and I said, "Get down, get down!" One little lad was too shocked to do as he was told, and I was terrified in case he attracted that man's attention again. I didn't know he was dead then. And finally, thankfully, people started to come in. It was over. At last it was over...

'We started shouting because we were still in the alcove and were afraid that people didn't know we were there. A nursery teacher, Linda, came in, and because at that stage, I suppose I must still have been thinking clearly, I shouted at her to get paper towels to put over the children's wounds. I even asked her to make sure that access to the gym was clear, because often cars parked in front of the entrance, and I knew it would need to be clear for the ambulances. But then, I found myself shaking uncontrollably, and feeling cold because I'd lost so much blood. I managed to tell Linda that I'd been shot in the chest, and she took off her own cardigan to cover me. I even asked her to tell Tony goodbye, and she said, "No, you tell him yourself!" That was absolutely the right thing for her to say, even though it must have been so hard for her to look at us in the state we were in. And it's an odd thought to recall now, but I kept saying "Oh my God, oh Jesus, Mary and Joseph!", which is really Catholic – and Mary would say, "I've lost my handbag. I don't know where my handbag is." What a pair we were as we lay there waiting, with me going, "Jesus, Mary and Joseph" in between her saying over and over that she had lost her handbag.

'None of us moved – not us, and not the children. We just waited for help. And eventually they moved the little ones off my legs, and got the injured ones out of the gym first. By then, some nurses and doctors had arrived from the surgery, and I remember four of them leaning over Mary and me. One was a doctor, and when I grabbed his tie, my arm was dripping blood. I panicked because I thought I was going to die – I remember begging him not to leave me, and saying what I thought might be my parting words.

'Eventually they put Mary into a neck brace, and got us into an ambulance. It's funny what you remember, but I noticed that the ambulance man had been smoking. When he touched my oxygen mask with the smell of cigarettes on his fingers, I thought I was going to be sick, and tried pushing him away. Of course, he didn't understand why I was pushing the mask away, but the smell of his hands, combined with the movement of the ambulance every time it went round a corner, really made me feel nauseous.

'When I look back, everything seemed to take for ever. It felt as if it took a long time first of all for help to come, until we wondered if people had forgotten us — although they hadn't, of course, it was just that it was such chaos. In fact, much later I learned that 'that man' had cut some of the telephone lines around the school. It had been a meticulously planned and executed operation. He hadn't intended us to be able to call for either the police or ambulance service. It seemed to take a long time to get the injured children out, and Mary and myself after that. And then those five or six miles to Stirling Royal Infirmary in the ambulance felt really long. Once there, we were rushed in, and immediately I was surrounded by a medical team. I discovered that one of the ambulance men had cut open my T-shirt in the gym, but I'd lost all my modesty and simply didn't care. I remember feeling tremendous guilt and responsibility for the children, because after all, I was the teacher, and the one in charge of them at the time of the attack. I was scared that they were going to knock me out before I had time to ask about them, and I desperately needed to know how they were. Actually, I was thinking that perhaps I wasn't going to make it through. If they knocked me out, then I would never know how the children were.

'And then, with a whole crowd of people around me doing things, I became aware of a calm voice coming from somewhere behind my head. He told me that I was going to be OK, and that although I was very ill, my injuries weren't life-threatening. Those were such important words, and they completely turned me round. I was going to live. I was going to live! The pendulum had swung in my favour, and I thanked God so much.

'Then they started asking me about the weapons that man had used, because they needed to know how to treat the children's injuries — and I described as best I could. They took me upstairs to a waiting bay before going into surgery and I knew that the children were in bays beside me. I remember asking a really nice doctor to tell me before he knocked me out how many were dead. I learned later that some children were airlifted to Glasgow, and others went to Falkirk as well as Stirling, so it seemed very chaotic. He told me what he thought was the current figure. And then I asked about Gwen. I don't know why I asked that. I knew she was dead but I needed to hear someone say, "Yes, she's dead." Although I'd seen it, I still couldn't believe it – until that moment. I had to believe it then.

'The one question I didn't ask at that time was *why*? That didn't come into it at all. It was just about survival, especially as the pain had really kicked in by then. I remember asking if I was likely to wake up with no arm. It's odd how you get degrees of normality. I just thought, I've got a chance to live. If I lose my arm, that's nothing. I'll still have my life.'

As Eileen was wheeled into surgery, one of the hospital team had been given the job of contacting her husband, Tony. He had been working at the office near Glasgow as normal, when he picked up the phone from someone at Stirling Hospital asking him if he was Mr Anthony Harrild. He listened in horror as they said that they were sorry to inform him that his wife had been shot, and that although her injuries were not life-threatening, she needed to see him. The news hit him like a sledge hammer. At first, he thought Eileen had perhaps been hit by something like a teenager's air gun, but by the time he was on his way to the infirmary, he had heard that there had been a serious shooting at Dunblane Primary School. His blood ran cold. Their children were there. Jennifer and Jack were pupils at the same school at which their mother was teaching that morning. Even when Tony arrived at the hospital, it wasn't clear exactly which class had been involved. Jack was in Primary 5. Tony knew that on one day of the week, his class went into PE first thing after assembly. Was it that morning? Please God it wasn't that morning . . .

He joined the group of distressed family members in the waiting room, while he waited for Eileen to be operated on. At this stage it was just emergency treatment to stitch up her chest, and wire and stabilize the bones in her arms and hand. Both bones in one arm had been completely shattered, 'like something you see in a cartoon, a big hole with a jagged wound all round it'. While Eileen slept after the operation, Tony frantically tried to get news about which children had been involved, desperate to know if Jennifer and Jack could possibly be amongst the injured. Meanwhile, unknown to either Tony or Eileen, their two older sons, Anthony and Andrew, had been taken into the Deputy Headmaster's office at Dunblane High School, and told that two adults were among the toll of people killed in the gym that morning. Their mother was the gym teacher. Their younger brother and sister were pupils at the primary school. That time of waiting and not knowing was a nightmare neither of those two young boys will forget for many years to come.

It was only much later in the day that Tony finally got news that both Jennifer and Jack were safe. That evening, he took all four children in to see their mum, so that they could reassure themselves that she was still with them, and on the road to recovery. Eileen remembers feeling distressed that they should see her in that state. In fact, for those youngsters, just seeing her was all they wanted and needed.

By that time, Eileen had learned the awful truth about the carnage of the day. Seventeen dead — Gwen, and sixteen children. Three teachers injured, along with twelve other children.

Eileen and Mary found themselves lying back to back in Intensive Care. Eileen vaguely noticed that there was a man sitting outside the door, and wondered who he was. In fact, he was a policeman posted there to protect them from intrusion by any uninvited visitors. What neither of them appreciated at the time was how the eyes and sympathy of the world were centred on Dunblane.

The following day when one of her friends came to visit, Eileen asked, "Did it get into the news?" 'I simply didn't have a clue,' Eileen remembers now, 'I just couldn't really believe that it had all been true. And every time the doctor or surgeon came in, I kept telling them what had happened. I just couldn't help myself wanting to speak about it all the time, as if I was trying come to terms with the realization that this had actually happened to me and the children. It was still so unbelievable.

'I couldn't sleep that first night, and when a nurse came in, I started talking about it again. It broke my heart to see that she couldn't stop crying. At first I thought she had a cold because her eyes were streaming, and she kept disappearing then coming back again. Later she told me how traumatic and difficult it had all been for the staff dealing with the casualties, because it upset them so much to see the state we were in. Until that moment, it hadn't occurred to me just how what we'd been through was touching so many people in different ways. She and I talked for ages, and it was at that point that I found myself wanting to understand *why*? Who was he? What had we ever done to him? None of it made sense. Why would he do this to innocent little children? It was such an act of evil, a human act of total evil. The enormity of it took a long time to sink in. Why had it happened? A lot of people ask where was God? Well, I have no doubt He was there. He was there in all the helpers and the medical staff who came to our aid. He was there for them as they saw what they had to see, knowing that they would have to cope with those horrible, disturbing images in their minds for the rest of their lives. They had to be really strong to do that – so brave to be able to face it all, then go on to show the calm courage that they did.

'I was in hospital for about two weeks initially, having a total of five operations in all, including one much later to graft bone from my hip into my shattered arm. Just prior to that operation, I was in a lot of pain because one of the poles was pressing on a nerve in my hand. The pain was dreadful, especially at night when however much pain control I had, I always found it hard to sleep. It was as if I were on a seesaw of reaction about what had happened to me. I kept telling myself how lucky I was to be here at all, that I should be grateful simply to be alive. And then I'd think why on earth should I be grateful? It should never have happened to me, nor to any of the others whose lives were shattered that day. And why should I thank my lucky stars to be alive, when rightfully I should be as healthy and fit as I ever was? My emotions were raw, my grief deep. I had seen a few of the children while we were all in hospital, when they popped up to see me. Some of the parents whose children had been wounded called in on me too, which I appreciated so much. I could see that just like Tony and me in our family, they were trying to keep themselves and their children on an even keel, hoping to get back to some sort of normal life as best they could. Their priority was just to get through each day, and support their youngsters as they coped with their injuries.

'At home, Tony was aiming to do much the same with our own children. I remember being very surprised when he sent the children back to the school the first day it re-opened. But he was right — trying to get family life back on to its usual footing, keep things as normal as possible, because if they were at home, what would they do? We had press people swarming around us like bees round a honeypot. Dunblane became a different place. It was swamped, and every time you opened your front door, there would be someone wanting to interview you. You were either locked out, or locked in. Journalists were going to the neighbours asking about us, and it wasn't pleasant. In hindsight, I realize that Tony was right to try and re-establish a normal routine as soon as possible.

'One thing which just overwhelmed me was when flowers started to arrive in my room from all over the world. People I didn't even know were sending me beautiful bouquets from India, Australia, everywhere. The room was covered with flowers, and lovely heartfelt notes which I still keep in my box upstairs. Unfortunately I couldn't reply because my arms and hand were too damaged, but their thought meant a lot to me. I knew in my heart that people really did care, and that was so important.

'I didn't see the inside of a church for about two months, but the canon kept coming along to talk to me, so that I became aware that everyone in the community was pulling together, supporting each other, and making sure that all the letters which poured in from around the world were answered. I was really moved to hear how people rallied round. They were wonderful. I shall never forget how once I got home, neighbours would just turn up at the door with a big lasagne for the children's tea. So useful, so practical, and so very thoughtful.

'But if you ask did the experience shake my faith, yes it did. How could God allow such a thing to happen to our children, our community? And I still don't know the answer to that. Perhaps there are some places you shouldn't go, some questions that have no answer – so I take the easy option because God gives me the free will to do that. But I have thought about the question of forgiveness. I'm not in a position to start considering forgiveness when the person who caused this awful hurt has never asked to be forgiven. He didn't seek our forgiveness, and even if he could, I don't think I would ever be able to forgive his evil.'

For Eileen, the next eighteen months seemed to be a long process of either having surgery or waiting for more operations, mostly because when they eventually did do the bone graft, she still had one arm much longer than the other, so they ended up having to re-operate to take more bone away. That was physically draining enough but she was also coping with the sudden illness of her much-loved father. She remembered that happy day just before the shooting when the whole family had been together, then recalled the shock in his face when he came to visit in her in hospital the day after she was hurt. His unexpected illness shook the family. Eileen found herself not only coping with the pain and worry of her own operations, but rushing across country to be strong for him and her mother. Her own family's needs and grief filled her time and energy, especially when her dad finally died. In the end, he died on the evening of the first day of the Cullen Inquiry, at which Eileen was the first person to give evidence. Her father had known how important Eileen's contribution was to that inquiry, and it was almost as if he hung on until he knew her evidence was safely given before he slipped away. It felt to her like a final act of love from the father she had always adored.

But while she was pre-occupied, the Snowdrop campaign, named after the flowers which were in bloom when the Dunblane children died, had not only been launched but was making sure its message was heard loud and clear across the land. The parents of the youngsters who died or were injured in the shooting were a small, strong, united group. They were articulate, intelligent and deter-mined, not afraid to take on the establishment. They had learned that everything 'that man' had done was legal. He had gone regularly to a local gun club, and *practised* the massacre he finally carried out. There was an anger, a determination locally that this should never be allowed to happen again. And if proper measures had been put in place after the earlier massacre in Hungerford, then their children might not have died. It took years, and a change of government before their demands were met, and handguns across the country were banned. It wouldn't bring the children back. It wouldn't touch the grief and pain felt not just by individual families, but by the whole wounded community of Dunblane. But it was a small, significant triumph – perhaps the only positive benefit to come out of the tragedy. This ban on handguns was too late for their youngsters, but it would almost certainly save the lives of countless others.

In the months that followed the loss of their children, Eileen got to know quite a few of the bereaved parents very well. She had been the last person to see their youngsters alive. They had so many questions, and more than anyone, she understood their grief, and their need to know.

Gradually, very gradually, on the surface at least, community life began to settle down again. Thoughts turned then to how the families, and the town, would like their youngsters' lives to be marked and remembered. Finally, it was agreed that a Garden of Remembrance would be created in the local cemetery, and a great deal of planning and care was put into exactly how it should be. The plaque that now stands at the entrance to the small, circular garden sums up their feelings and aims for this special place.

This garden is dedicated to the memory of our beloved children and their dear teacher whose lives were taken so tragically on 13th March, 1996, at Dunblane Primary School. We treasure them for all they were, and remember that they hold an unique and precious place in the hearts of those who love them.

Gwen Mayor, Emma, Charlotte, Ross, Mhairi, Abigail, Sophie, Joanna, Megan, Victoria, Melissa, Kevin, David, Brett, Emily, John, Hannah

Forever loved and remembered

Each headstone lovingly and individually reflects the character of the child to which it is dedicated. Snowdrops, rabbits and even Thomas the Tank Engine are endearingly carved into the stone. Small soft toys sit grinning cheekily, just as those small girls and boys grinned and laughed during their short, happy lives. And the carefully worded inscriptions must have been impossibly hard to decide upon when there was so much to say that needed to be captured in a few short phrases. 'To our golden boy,' says one, 'May he run, skip, giggle and play forever.' The garden today is beautiful – peaceful, fitting, dignified, affectionate, and heartstoppingly sad.

The churches of the town each made their own act of remembrance. In Eileen's Holy Family Catholic church, the parishioners erected a thoughtful and stunningly vibrant stained glass window, which moves from darkness into light. It shows the Holy Spirit as a flight of sixteen doves, each representing one of the children who lost their lives. They are linked together by a daisy chain, the symbol of childhood and innocence, and are guided towards the light by a larger dove representing their teacher, Gwen. They follow her in alphabetical order, as she might have called them forward in class. Each bird has a slightly different shape, colour and flower in its beak, illustrating the individual personality of each child, and the presence which they leave with us. Snowflakes drift to the ground symbolizing the teachers and children who were injured. Where they fall, the shoots of new snowdrops start to grow. The snowdrop, so closely associated with the Dunblane tragedy, is a token of consolation during the dark winter days, and a promise of spring to come.

Eileen sees that window every time she goes to worship there. And she sees in the church too one of the youngsters who was badly wounded, but who is now an altar boy. Seeing him brings her comfort and encouragement. Just as the physical wounds are slowly healing, so broken hearts are beginning to be pieced back together, never quite the same again, but with hope among the painful memories. Five years on, Eileen too is picking up the strands of her life.

'I'm so aware now of how fragile everything is, and that in the blink of an eye, it can change so dramatically. It's made me more protective of my own children, terrified that something might happen to them. I know that they're growing up, and need to go and spread their wings, and I have to ask Jennifer and Jack to bear with me. I just never thought that what did happen could happen. You never know what's round the corner, do you?

'As a family, we're closer now than ever – and we really value the support of the people we know in Dunblane. We've stuck together and gained strength from each other because we needed it. And it means a lot to me to see Mary often. We are the only two who really understand how we feel about what we went through.

'Most of all, I strive to be normal, the way I always was. Some people know me now simply because I was the teacher shot at Dunblane. I don't like that. It happened to me, but it isn't all that I am.'

Because Eileen no longer has the strength in her arms to lift equipment or support children, she was never able to go back to the work she loved as a PE teacher. She tried a part-time administrative post in the Education Office, and although that meant her visiting schools during her work, she missed close contact with the children. 'I love their honesty and enthusiasm,' she says. 'I'm young enough to make a fresh start, do something different, but I don't yet know what that might be. For now, my family is my life. Perhaps in a few months, I'll start brushing up my skills, and see what else I can do.'

In the meantime, the primary school has been re-constructed and re-opened, and life goes in Dunblane. But what happened there, and the lessons to be learned from it, must never be forgotten, just as the sixteen small girls and boys who died will always be remembered. Their short lives were precious and valued. The way they looked, laughed, cried, moved and hugged is indelibly etched on the hearts of the families who brought them into the world, and loved them so dearly. Perhaps Winnie the Pooh, quoted on the tombstone of one of the little boys who died, says it best of all:

When I was one
I had just begun.
When I was two

I was nearly new.
When I was three
I was hardly me.
When I was four
I was not much more.
When I was five
I was just alive.
But now I am six
I'm as clever as clever,
So I think I'll be six now
For ever and ever.

Blaise

Amongst Irish Catholic families, there's an expression you'll sometimes hear which carries with it a stigma of shame and failure.
'Spoilt Priest' is the term used to describe a man if after years of
living as a monk or a priest, he decides the religious life is no longer
right for him. Blaise made just such a decision after four years in a
monastery, when he left because he felt unable to take his Solemn
Vows to become a monk. His story of devotion, spiritual heights,
depths and soul searching is deeply touching and very human.

His Christian name was Peter when as a young boy his mother
decided that her son's salvation, both educationally and spiritually,
lay with the Irish Christian Brothers. 'Coax it into them, or beat it
into them – but do the job' was the unofficial motto of the Christian
Brothers, and certainly their attempts to instil education into Peter
relied more on brute force than mental stimulation. When he
scraped into the sixth form, he found himself surrounded by fellow
pupils who had a clear idea of the career paths before them. They
were planning an apprenticeship at the local shipyards or car-
building company, or perhaps the more academic route towards
becoming an accountant or doctor. Peter's future was blank, and his
ambition once in the sixth form stretched no further than the joint

events held with the local girls' convent school. In fact, as the hormones kicked in, so did his determination to meet girls whenever possible – at the Friday Night Club, the Debating Society, and anywhere else that girls might be. As his social life blossomed, studies floundered, and after fluffing his A Levels, he chose to use his muscles rather than his brain for a while. He took up landscaping, which is why at the age of eighteen, he found himself working in the Lake District for a few weeks at a place where the Davies family had stayed on holiday over the years – a convent called Boarbank Hall, a convalescent home and convent run by Augustinian nuns. It was there that the idea of becoming a priest first crept up on him when, in between gardening and rain showers, Peter began chatting to a young nun called Sister Dympna. He made several interesting discoveries about her – firstly, that she was 'not Irish, and only a few years younger than God himself'! Secondly, entering the convent hadn't dimmed her love of football and 'indie music', passions which she shared with Peter. Thirdly, becoming a nun had done nothing to dampen her zest for life and her sharp sense of humour. Amongst conversations about the music they loved, and the teams they supported, they managed to fit in quite a bit of discussion about God, life and the universe. By the time he left Boarbank, Peter had begun to realize that Sister Dympna had allowed him to glimpse an alternative yet very accessible option for life.

'I suppose there were several things which drew me to the priesthood. Firstly, priests had been an everyday part of my life as I grew up. It wasn't unusual to find the local priest or Benedictine monk in our house, as much a part of the furniture as the rest of us as he guzzled father's whisky. But it was a respectable position within the community, and in many ways I recognized a sense of heroism in the role of the priest because of everything they have to sacrifice in order to serve their community. Apart from that, such a choice would give me a sense of direction at a time when I had no other idea of direction at all. Ultimately, though, what it came down to was a call from God. If I hadn't believed that deep within me I was being called by a power much higher than myself, then I could never have sustained my commitment to it for so many years. It wasn't the lifestyle that attracted me at all — in fact, quite the opposite. It just felt as if there was a nagging, gnawing feeling inside me to which I had to respond. It was like have a perpetually running nose — eventually you have to blow it. No matter how much I tried to deny it, the awkwardness, the incessant tap, tap, tapping on the back of my mind hour after hour was impossible to ignore. You have to remember too that at this stage in my life, I had hardly tasted the material world. I had grown up with constant discipline both at home and school, and so progression to a seminary or monastery seemed perfectly natural.

'I remember my father saying to me one night that he thought I was a loner, which had never occurred to me before. In fact, the word "monk" comes from the Greek word, "monos", which means "alone". I recognized that I enjoyed my own company, and felt quite independent and self-sufficient when on my own. Perhaps because of that, I felt that the opportunity to be self-sufficient within the structure of religious life would enable me to be both dynamic and creative.

'Mind you, it wasn't an idea which I accepted easily. I remember returning from Boarbank and making a beeline for the pub with a pal of mine and getting blind drunk trying to talk myself out of it! I had a great social life. I enjoyed football. With all my friends, I liked going to pubs, clubs and parties. The very thought of leaving that all behind to become a priest was very difficult to accept. The idea thumped me between the eyes, and for several days I felt as if I'd been given terrible news, like someone diagnosed with a life-threatening illness.

'The Scriptures talk about how there will come a time when

you will have a belt tied around your waist, and you will be led to somewhere you'd rather not go. That's how I felt. I knew that God had come into my somewhat dysfunctional life, to take me somewhere beyond my control. There's a saying in religious life, "Don't swim against the tide – just go with the flow". In the end, that's exactly what I did. As soon as my mind began to conceptualize the idea of letting go and allowing the flow to carry me, I found myself at great peace. All of a sudden, from the most unexpected quarter, I knew where I wanted to go. It was too good to be true.

'Some might think that such a decision is inevitable after the kind of traditional, strict Catholic upbringing I'd been through – that I must have been running away, escaping life. But there is also a thought in Catholic teaching that grace builds on nature. God works with the materials He has at hand. He certainly did with me.

'I remember my mum was sitting on her bed doing her hair when I came in to tell her that I wanted to become a Benedictine – although honestly, at that time, I really wasn't sure exactly what that meant. She replied in a flash, "No, no, you can't! You've got to be intellectual to become a Benedictine." That was it, no more discussion – so I went away thinking all right, I'll be a diocesan priest then!

'Mum showed neither enthusiasm nor disapproval. She probably thought I was just going through a fad, like punk music, the Beatles, blue hair, trainers, jeans or whatever. Then she mentioned to someone that I'd talked about being a Benedictine monk, which wouldn't be at all appropriate as I wasn't intellectual, and the friend told her that she knew someone whose only O Level was in woodwork, and he was as thick as two short planks – yet he was a monk at Ampleforth! Before I knew it, I arrived back from work one evening, to find the sitting room full of priests. Now, I was well used to the odd priest or Benedictine popping in for a drink with Dad every now and then, but this gathering was obviously different.

I sat chatting to first one priest, then another – and out of their pockets, one by one, each of them would pull out a little Catholic Truth Society pamphlet. They are small twenty-page pamphlets on the favourite saints like St Peter and St Paul, on marriage, making your first Holy Communion, and about the priesthood. By the end of the evening, I had about six copies of the pamphlet on St Benedict. One of the priests there, Father David O'Brien who's a Benedictine, said, "Of course, you do realize we're monks, don't you?" Well, that came as such a shock to me. Monks! All I knew about them before that was that they wore black corduroy trousers! I flew upstairs and said to God, "Look, you've got to get me out of this. Something in the back of my head is saying I want to become a Benedictine, and now you throw this one at me! They're monks!" I realized then that there was only a fifty/fifty chance if I joined them that I would ever end up in a parish. My dream was to go back and work in Liverpool, which at that time, at the height of the recession in the eighties, was in a bad way, with the Toxteth Riots in the headlines. Suddenly, these Benedictines were telling me that only a few of them worked in parishes. The rest stay in the monastery. Their monastery at Ampleforth is a bit like the Halifax Building Society, where the head office is in North Yorkshire, but they have branches as well. I discovered that training to become a monk took place at the monastery, then you might be sent away to Oxford, or perhaps abroad, to study theology, before coming back to do a bit of teaching in the boys' school attached to the Abbey. If I took that route, I was more likely to end up a teacher than at work in a parish – and I knew that my ultimate plan was to come back to Liverpool.

'Nevertheless, in spite of all my reservations, I decided to make the trip to Ampleforth. It was 13 December 1984, and even now, I remember it vividly. I had been through a period of oscillating between what I felt God was calling me to do, and my own feelings about the future, when one of the monks said he'd ring up the Guest Master at Ampleforth, Father Cyril, so that I could visit for a weekend. That Friday afternoon, I finished work, got changed, packed a bag and got the train to York where I was met by Father Cyril. You have to remember that I had grown up in the rather run-down city of Liverpool. As I got into the car with Father Cyril, he drove me twenty-three miles north of York into the most spectacular countryside. It was one of those crystal clear crisp winter days as I looked across the valley towards the Abbey. Sunlight was catching the sandstone of the abbey church and monastery as they dominated the lush green valley with its smattering of rugby posts. It was so spectacular, stoic and very English. It was the first time I'd ever seen a monastery. Like most people in this country, I thought monks belonged to a remote mediaeval period in France or Germany, and here it was in glorious technicolor.

'Once inside the monastery, I was put in what they call a horse box, a guest room which was very small and sparsely furnished. There was something about the atmosphere that caught me though – the dark corridor, the wooden floorboards, and the smell as I went in, very male – no frills, just functional, which was great for me. Most of all, what sold the place to me was the calefactory, which means the "warming room", dating back to mediaeval times when it was a place where monks could come to warm themselves after a day in the fields. Nowadays, it's a sitting room and social area for the brothers. It was four o'clock in the afternoon, tea time and between four and five o'clock is what they call "being in community" when the brothers all come in for conversation, a cup of tea, and to read the papers. The sun was just going down. I could hear the clatter of rugby boots as the school boys went back to their houses. I sat there in front of a roaring fire as the monks came in, not batting an eyelid to see me there. No effusive welcomes, no raised eyebrows. It was just as though I'd always been there. They were carving up pieces of bread, toasting them in front of the fire with long forks, before eating them with jam and butter. I just thought what a wonderful life it was. Then several youngish monks came in, and the atmosphere felt like a cross between a sixth form common room and a football changing room with its banter, leg-pulling and chat. They all seemed like really cool blokes, not at all hassled like the monks I'd met in Liverpool. I was overwhelmed with a sense of home-coming, and the knowledge that I could be very happy there.

'That weekend, they left me alone a lot. All the monks I spoke to quite plainly enjoyed the fulfilling and energizing lifestyle they had there. They were very matter-of-fact about it all. Then I had an interview with two wise old monks, one very round and jolly, the other quite stern. They went through the usual questions, like "Do you pray? What do you pray for? What's your favourite hymn? Why do you want to become a monk?" I managed to answer all those queries reasonably well, but it was the last question Father Benet threw at me just as I was leaving that I remember most. He said, "Have you ever been in love?" That floored me, so I just replied, "Not with you, Father," and left. Someone told me much later that if I had answered "Yes", the next question would probably have been, "What's it like?"

'Anyway, I was delighted to be offered a place in the novitiate that September. Six of us joined at the same time. For the first week we were on what is called "postulants' retreat", where we remained in our civvy clothes, but attended the daily services. Some were in Latin with traditional Gregorian chants — very haunting. The fact that the words were in Latin was part of the mystique for me. With its own metre and rhythm, it felt almost like a mantra.

'At the end of that first week, there was a clothing ceremony — and then you hand the Abbot a list of five saints' names which you think you might like to take on as you join the monastery. As there were already a hundred monks at Ampleforth, you had to select a name which hadn't already been chosen, so it was a bit limiting. St Blaise, I discovered, was the patron saint of sore throats, Dubrovnic and Bradford! He was an eighth-century saint put to death by the Emperor of the time. On the way to his execution, a mother brought to him her son who was choking to death on a fish bone. St Blaise blessed him and cured him of the ailment. He's been the patron saint of sore throats ever since! I found that I really didn't mind losing my own name – Peter Davies had always seemed rather boring. The name Blaise felt much more exotic – so I just thought, that's it, and thankfully the Abbot chose it as well!

'I remember after the clothing ceremony, one of the first Saturdays as a novice was spent cleaning toilets, or other menial domestic work like polishing the choir stalls or ironing vestments. Have you ever seen a habit clogged with wax? It was while I was cleaning toilets on my first Saturday that I thought about what I was missing in the outside world. I realized that the previous week at three o'clock I had been standing on the Kop at Anfield, because football and Liverpool F.C. had always been my great passion. Apart from that I found I was missing my brother, and quite a few of my friends. I managed to get round the problem of hearing about Liverpool games through a monk called Father David who had once been based in a parish in Liverpool. When he came in for Vespers on Saturday evenings he would use the fingers on one hand to show how many goals Liverpool scored, and the other to show the score of the opposition. So my ability to sing with gusto on Saturday evenings was dependent on what the score was!

'In fact, I look back now to see that there's a whole period of my life between 1985 and 1990 when events took place that I only discovered when I came out – including the whole music scene. The first time I went home, I got off at Lime Street where there was a long queue of kids outside the Royal Court Theatre. I went up to a girl who was wearing a stripey shirt and a beret, and asked who was playing there that night. She said, "Curiosity Killed the Cat." So I said, "I was only asking!" I didn't realize that was the name of the group!

'In many ways though, whatever you missed in the outside world, you discovered a new world within the walls of the monastery. There was an initial teething period as I settled into the rhythm of the day. People might say that monastic life is a very wooden, structured routine. In fact, I found it rather comforting. After a while, it was reassuring to know exactly where I was at what time of the day. From nine o'clock every evening until Compline at nine the next morning, was the *Sumuum Silencium* – the Grand Silence – when no one spoke to each other. A bell would go at half past five in the morning, when we'd get up, have a wash, put on our habits, then go down for Matins at 6 a.m. Then from half past six until quarter past seven was the time for private prayer. My favourite place for doing that was in my stall. Each brother has an allocated space in the stalls, where we'd sit with our hoods up which was a sign that either we were in prayer, or didn't want to be disturbed. I enjoyed that time, especially in the early morning when over my habit I would wear a cowl which was like a big round parachute of cloth. I would pull up my hood, then wrap myself round with the cowl so that it felt very cosy. Breakfast would be at eight, in silence because we were still "in *Sumuum*" until nine. Even though we couldn't speak, we had a sign language for useful things like "Pass the marmalade" and "Can I have some sugar please?"

'At nine o'clock, many of the monks would go off to take classes in the school, while the novices would have their own lessons in philosophy, scripture, church history and Latin. To be surrounded by so many articulate, well-read, incredibly learned, intelligent men who have a passion for faith, literature, language and the classics was wonderful for me. At school, the Christian Brothers had made me believe I didn't have a brain in my head. The great thing about the Benedictines, though, is that they are wonderful educators, using suggestion rather than brute force. It wasn't a chore, it was a way of life, a process of osmosis — I suddenly realized I wasn't as thick as I believed myself to be! Anyway, they decided that I had probably just been a lazy so-and-so at school, so I should take A levels in history, politics and RE as well as my normal round of theological studies.

'But of all the things I learned at Ampleforth, the most important was learning to pray. Before that time, prayer for me had always meant reciting by heart the Lord's Prayer, Hail Mary and other devotional prayers. Suddenly I was being taught about meditation and mental prayer. There was a period between tea at four and Vespers at six when we were expected to do three-quarters of an hour of *lectio divina* or spiritual reading, and a quarter of an hour of mental prayer — and I remember getting a rollicking from the Novice Master when he found me down in the crypt struggling through *Mere Christianity* by C.S. Lewis, relying on my rosary beads. I was told that to use the rosary like that was effectively the same as using a crutch. If you're a monk, you're supposed to be "professional" at praying. You have to master, and know you can rely on, your own mental prayer. It took me a long time. I really didn't understand at the start what he was saying to me. Then, one day it clicked. It's very difficult for me to describe what it felt like, but that first year at Ampleforth was undoubtedly the happiest of my whole life. I found that I was able to pray in such a way that I felt the incredible presence of God. I believe I came as close to God as you can possibly be whilst here on earth. There was such a sense of closeness between God and myself. In the deepest form of prayer, you don't rely on words or concepts. You can just be still, and be with God. The psalm says, "Be alone and rest my soul." That's just what it was like — almost as if you're in the presence of the most beautiful person with whom you are deeply in love. I just sat there in the presence, not needing to say anything. You don't need to rely on stimulants, such as thinking about flowers, sunshine, blue skies, words from the Scripture, or a wonderful painting – I simply focused on the all-encompassing presence of God who loved me unconditionally. I was just there, and at one with Him. For about eighteen months, perhaps two years, that was my experience of prayer. It was truly wonderful.

'But I realize that when someone looks so tangibly as if they are close to God, they have something which can create a sort of prejudice amongst others who wonder what's so special about them. I look back to recognize that one of the worst things about me then was that I had become incredibly arrogant.

'While you're in the novitiate, you are called every three months to "a perseverance", which is when you go before the Novice Master to discuss what you think of all the other novices. Then you're called back in again a second time to hear what everyone else has said about you. At that time, I was having such incredibly powerful experiences – wonderfully close meditation to the extent that I only had to read for five minutes, then spent the rest of the time in prayer when it was just me and God. I had a hot-line – and something of that must have conveyed itself to the others. I went in to see the Novice Master after my first three months thinking this is easy, great, I love this monastic life. Straight away, he said, "Everybody seems to think you're full of yourself, arrogant, can't be told anything. There are all sorts of people here – a Vietnamese refugee who's travelled half way round the world, a trained doctor, a former teacher – and according to you, you know more about religion, politics, everything, than they do." It was a painfully honest and humiliating experience. I came out reeling. Just when I felt so close to God, I realized that I was most far away from the people with whom I was living. "Pride comes before a fall", as it were.

'After three perseverances, the monastery can decide to ask you to leave if they feel you're getting in the way of the other novices, and plainly not suited to the monastic life. The novitiate is very tough, some would say "the bloodier the better". Certainly there is no way you could survive it if God didn't want you to. Your health would go, for a start. Throughout my time in the novitiate there were instances of guys who desperately wanted to be monks, but who couldn't stand the physical challenge of it. Lent was always a particularly grim time, "a refiner's fire", the ultimate test because the liturgy becomes very routine, with no feast days to break the monotony. We would suggest our own list of restrictions or devotions, like fasting, or reading an extra book. That list would be agreed by both the Abbot and the novice, and those devotions would be added to our manual labour tasks which were very hard during the dark, dingy days of February.

'At the end of our first year, we could take Simple Vows of Obedience, Stability and *Conversatio Morum* for a period of three years. The Vow of Obedience means agreeing to obey the instructions of an Abbot. By taking the Vow of Stability, you attach yourself to life in and with a particular monastic community. The Vow of *Conversatio Morum* is best translated as Conversion of Manners, and involves a commitment to changing your way of life each day to the Rule of St Benedict and the Gospels. The vow implicitly includes poverty and celibacy.

'The normal plan would be to take Simple Vows at the end of the first year, then take Solemn Vows three years later. You could then also choose to be ordained as a priest at that point, although many monks decide not to take that step because they feel that for them it's a distraction.

'After taking my Simple Vows, I was still in the novitiate, so things were pretty much as they had been in the first year, except that for two evenings a week we were able to go in and mix with other members of the community. There is a novitiate gallery right at the top of the monastery, which is where we slept separately from the main part of the monastery. In fact, we had no real contact with the rest of the community in the monastery until we came out of the novitiate. That was due to happen at the end of my second year, but it was after my first year, and the taking of my Simple Vows, that things began to fall apart for me.

'I remember the night the bottom fell out of my world. I was studying round the clock for my A Levels, and a whole world of education was opening up for me – perhaps going to Oxford to do a degree in Politics and Economics. I had my future mapped out, a great white hope of what I was going to become. I saw myself as a future House Master at Ampleforth, and who knew what eventually – maybe even Abbot? I felt really good about myself, and believed I had a position of worth within the community. I recognize now that I was too proud, even arrogant. And Ampleforth seemed to me to be such a "happening place". Everything was buzzing. Our former Abbot, Basil Hume, had gone on to become Cardinal, and was talking to kings, queens and politicians. We were running one of the top public schools which was not just successful but had a great atmosphere. Every year, about half a dozen people were applying to join our novitiate, at a time when numbers were dropping off elsewhere in the country. And we had a great Abbot, Father Patrick, who was like a dad. In fact, Abba means "daddy" – and Father Patrick was a real father figure, and a very saintly man. If ever you had troubles, you could go to him. Anyway, I felt all of a sudden that I had arrived. I was enjoying reading and education, and studying for my A Levels, and I was surrounded by a lot of young monks in a place with great vision.

'I suppose what happened was that I began to believe the dream, and started to want it too much. And I was growing up as well. There was a bit of internal strife going on within the novitiate at the time too, so I felt I was running it – or at least, I felt I *ought* to be running it. I was desperately studying for my A Levels, plus packing in all my monastic studies and everything else. In the end, it was a bit like a pressure cooker.

'It was then that I was allowed to go back home to Liverpool for the first time in two years. I stepped back into that wonderful, fantastic city, and felt overwhelmingly happy to be there. I was only home for about five days, but I had a gut feeling that real life was happening here, rather than in the monastery. Then I met a couple of friends that I'd known from school, and was amazed at everything they'd experienced. When I'd last seen them, they'd been teenagers in the first throws of infatuations and girlfriends. Now they were twenty-three year olds who'd got their university degrees, interesting careers, and had settled down as husbands. What hit me was how much they'd matured. I had matured in other ways, but when it came to relationships, their lives had really moved on. I found myself sitting in a pub having an in-depth, adult conversation with a nice young lady who had been out in Russia studying at the time when Chernobyl had blown up — someone whose health could have been at risk, who had gone through a traumatic time which she felt she could talk about to me. It was so wonderful to listen and share conversation with her. I wanted to go on spending time like that, sharing the depth of our experience and feelings. I was used to a totally male environment, like the football changing room, yet here I discovered a different type of human companionship with women, who, after all, made up half of the world's population! In a flash, I realized that I was denying myself this enjoyable companionship. It felt like a seed that had lain dormant for two years which had suddenly been sprinkled with water — and bang! Out of nowhere comes new life! A new door had opened to a chamber inside me that I had not seen before — and I couldn't close it again.

'When I got back to Ampleforth, I was in turmoil, not knowing where to turn. It was coming up to the end of August, when there was a retreat and chapter – in other words, a kind of AGM for all the monks, when everyone would gather together to pray, review the year, and plan the future. And I was going through my own personal review, a long process of mental gymnastics because I felt under unbearable pressure to leave. I was convinced that I was heading for a complete breakdown. I lost my ability to pray, which was immensely painful. I never lost my faith in God though. I never could because of those first eighteen months at Ampleforth when I had met God so intimately. That I will always take with me.

'I had been in touch with my mother to say that I was almost certainly going to leave. Her reaction was instant. If I left, I could not come home. She believed that my ultimate destiny lay in becoming a monk or a priest, and that therefore it would be wrong for me to leave. She felt I should stay and work it through.

'My turmoil went on for about two or three months, before finally around Christmas I reached such a turning point that I knew I had to go and talk to the Abbot. He was fantastic. He's such a holy man with an onerous responsibility on his shoulders, because St Benedict says that on the Day of Judgement, he will have to give an account of every soul he has had in his charge. We novices always felt his fatherly love for us.

'Before that meeting on Christmas Eve, I had been through weeks of the dark night of the soul, thinking that the Simple Vows I had taken lacked a sense of permanence. I knew I couldn't go through the next two years until my Simple Vows ran out feeling so uncertain of my calling. I had to leave. The Abbot challenged me by saying that during my Simple Vows, in front of my friends, family, and the community, I had promised to give God three years in that place. That didn't mean one year and so many days – it meant three years. He said that if after three years, I still felt I needed to leave, I could go with his blessing, but how could I know what life decision might come along within my time left at Ampleforth? I had to trust my powers of resolve and commitment. If I walked out now, how could I ever trust myself in the future? In a letter the Abbot wrote me later, he quoted a line from *A Man for All Seasons*. It was the moment when Thomas More confronts Roper, his son-in-law, who has demonstrated conflicting allegiances between Henry VIII and Rome. More simply states, "Let's hope that when your head stops spinning, it's pointing in the right direction." Well, my mind was certainly spinning when I left the Abbot that evening. I didn't want to hear what he said to me, and I felt so demoralized. Rationally I understood his words, but emotionally I did not want to accept them. I went back up to my room having decided to ring my brother and ask him to pick me up. Then I lay down on my bed, and thought I'll ring him after I've had a sleep. The next thing I knew the bell was ringing for Vespers. It's true what they say about when life gets you down, it is usually the routine of work that pulls you through. I didn't have time to ring my brother that night. In the end, I didn't get round to ringing him at all.

'I had been at Ampleforth for two and a quarter years by the time I had that meeting with the Abbot. In order to fulfil my commitment to three years after my Simple Vows in the monastery, I had to stay for another year and nine months. The Abbot requested that I should not discuss my decision to leave with anyone except my Spiritual Director during that time in case it undermined the atmosphere within the community. In fact, it was always true in the monastery that you never knew that someone had left until you noticed there was a gap in the choir.

'Throughout that remaining time, I kept a piece of paper on which I counted off the days. At this stage, I was out of the novitiate, running prayer groups in the sixth formers' rooms – and I was only a few years older than them myself! Then I used to come back to my silent cell in the monastery, and long for someone to ask if I'd had a bad day, or share a meal, have a chat, be a companion . . .

'When you live in a totally male environment in a celibate state, the longing for female company can become overwhelming. For those guys who feel that monastic life or priesthood is not for them and leave the confines of a seminary or monastery, the answer is often to get out in the world and do some other form of pastoral work. But then because they've got to their twenties without ever had the experience of being with women, they fall into the arms of the first one they meet, completely and utterly in love. It's one hell of a drug, very hypnotic. Because of the discipline of monastic life, everything looks more polarized. The trees seem greener, the sky bluer, the beauty of the scenery at sunset particularly powerful. But the beauty of another person is all the more striking. And if you have been through a Christian Brothers' school, then straight into monastic life, with all its routine and stoic instruction, then to come across the loveliness of a human relationship with a woman seemed so wonderful and disarming, as if the seams of your being were being plucked away, ripped apart. I felt like jelly, unable to think, drunk with the thought of being in love with another human being.

'My four years should have been up in September, but in the end the Abbot said that I could be granted leave of absence from 25 June 1989, which was the day when my fellow novices Benjamin, Cuthbert, James and Barnabus were to be ordained as deacons, which is one stage before priesthood. They had all taken their Solemn Vows by this time.

'That ceremony was so emotional for me. I knew it was my last day there, but my brother monks had no idea. At the end of the ceremony, everyone went off for the traditional bunfight of tea and cakes — and I went and got my box, and went out through the infirmary to meet my brother, who had come to take me home.

'In that box was the sum total of my possessions — clothes which I'd arrived in four years earlier which now looked ridiculously out of date. I was given £10 by the Procurator, which was the single train fare back to Liverpool's Lime Street Station and apart from the National Insurance contributions in my name, that was all I had in the world. I spent that £10 on Guinness in a pub about six miles away. I can't tell you how wonderful it tasted. I fell asleep in the car, and the next thing I knew we were coming down by the docks in Liverpool. Actually, I felt quite odd about that homecoming, because one of the few people I had spoken to about my decision to leave was Cardinal Basil Hume. He had been Abbot at Ampleforth, and always thought of us as his family. He often came back for a holiday during which time we would sometimes go for walks, and chat about the progress of our respective football teams. He knew what I would be facing on my return. He understood very well, because his own father had once told him, "It takes a great man to enter the monastery. It takes a greater man to leave."

'We both knew of that saying "a spoilt priest". In traditional urban Irish Catholicism, from the moment you go into the seminary, that's it – you're a priest. To leave is tantamount to walking out on a marriage. There was a tremendous stigma attached to it. I knew my mother felt that deeply – and Cardinal Hume recognized it too. That's why he offered to let me come and stay in his house at Westminster while I got myself together.

'I bore that offer in mind as I went back home to be given a less than rapturous reception – the cold shoulder, in fact. Fortunately, my parents had moved parishes, so not everyone in the church knew that I was ex-Brother Blaise, the ex-Ampleforth monk. Things were difficult at home. My dad was pleased to see me, as was my brother because I've always been close to him. But my mother had a mixture of feelings, dominated by her worry that at the age of twenty-four, with all my contemporaries now through university with careers settled in front of them, I was still wondering what on earth I could do with my life! I came out without a penny to my name. I didn't even have clothes except some my brother lent me so that I could start gardening again.

'In October, though, everything changed when I finally went off to Leeds University to take a degree in Business Studies and the Media. The odd thing was that I was still officially in vows, because the Abbot had said that the door would be kept open in case I ever felt I wanted to return to the monastic life. When I applied to university, I had no photographs for the form, so sent off an old snapshot of me in my dog collar. When I first arrived, they had allocated me to the Girls' Hall, because they assumed the name Blaise belonged to a girl! After that, when they saw the photograph, they decided that I must be linked to the chaplaincy. Just as I wanted to forget my past, I found that there would be a knock on the door and I'd open it to find a whole string of women in ballgowns crying! They thought I was the Assistant Chaplain, and wanted to tell me how their boyfriends had dumped them. I had a whale of a time, even though I probably had the least knowledge of relationships out of all the students there!

'I had made myself a promise while I was sitting in my monastic cell. I decided that having given the prime years of my youth to God, that at the age of twenty-four I was going to take every opportunity that came my way. I don't know if my thinking was precise enough to define hedonistic pleasure – but whether the opportunity was to bungee or parachute jump, to work in America, or play football, I would give it a go if the chance presented itself. I obviously drew attention to myself, because I can remember my Head of Business Studies saying that he wrote off my first two years at university because I obviously had a lot of catching up to do!

'One of the reasons why I chose Leeds University was that my friend, Father David Smith, was the University Chaplain there. I didn't realize until much later that the Abbot had written to Dave asking him to look after me. In fact, we ended up very close friends.

The irony was that another one of his responsibilities was as Vocations Director for the Diocese of Leeds – in other words, he was recruiting guys for the priesthood, at the same time as supporting me when I left it! Through him, I ended up sharing a house in Leeds not just with men like me who were leaving the priesthood, but others who were going on to take up the life of a priest. It was quite bizarre really.

'Anyway, I was having a wonderful time, enjoying the social life, the football, the girlfriends and everything else that went with it. And on the other hand, there was Dave Smith who would occasionally say to me, "You know, you're still fighting the priesthood."

'And in many ways, I was. I knew that the decision was by no means finished. I suppose it's a Catholic thing, that there are three options in life. One is to get married, which 99% of us do. The second is the single life, and the third is the monastic life or priesthood. And because of that, for many years after leaving the religious life, you can't quite break away. I challenge anyone, man or woman, who's made that choice to say that they have never had hankerings and thoughts about going back. Cardinal Hume, who became a very good friend once I left Ampleforth, often had this knowing look about him, as if I was really running away, but that the priesthood would get me in the end. In honesty, that thought was always at the back of my mind when I got into a relationship with a girlfriend – almost, as Princess Diana said, as if there was a third presence in the relationship – in my case, not a person, but the pull of priesthood. Sometimes, I would even use it as an excuse if I was too cowardly to finish a relationship in a more honest way – I would tell a girl that I was thinking of going back to being a priest. It must have been hard for her, because it wasn't as if there was another woman there whose face she could slap!

'In the end, because I was unsure exactly what work I was destined to do, I found myself drawn back to Ampleforth to take up the post of their Public Relations Officer. It is a common experience amongst ex-seminarians and ex-monks to find themselves drawn back to the place they have left. In fact, it is sometimes called "the Hound of Heaven" which is barking behind you, herding you back into the seminary again – and for me, it certainly barked for a good few years, even until quite recently. I wasn't one of the brothers any more, but I worked closely with them. I found the place very changed in the time I'd been away. It had become more PLC, more corporate than when I'd been there previously. It simply didn't have the same buzz for me that I'd felt in the eighties. Finally, that decided it for me. I ended up setting up my own business – because in terms of being employed by other people, how do you describe to your potential employer the gap of five years on your CV while you were in a monastery? I realized that I came from a family of little entrepreneurs and business people, so in setting up my own website design business, I ended up some time later living and working in Altrincham on the outskirts of Manchester.

'One night there, while I was queuing up outside a wine bar, I met a girl called Jo. She was actually going out with a friend of mine, but apparently, I learned later, she quite liked me. When eventually our mutual friend got married, I asked her to come to the wedding with me. That night we retired to the same wine bar where we'd first met, and with a live band playing and fun and chatter all round us, I realized I couldn't go into a serious relationship with her without resolving something. So after a while, I said, "I've got something to confess to you." I told her that I had trained as a monk for four years, and that it had been a big stumbling block both for me, and for girls I had known, when it came to relationships. She was completely unperturbed, because it turned out that her own father had trained as a priest earlier in his life as well! And that was the start.

'On 26 May 2000, ten years after leaving Ampleforth, Jo and I were married at our local church, St Vincent's, and a number of the Ampleforth monks, my good friends Justin, Matthew and Paul, were involved in performing the ceremony. I hadn't rushed into anything. Those words of the Abbot had stayed with me – "Let's hope when your head stops spinning, it's pointing in the right direction." I knew how important it was to make the right decision and stick by it. That advice has stood me in good stead.

'There is such rightness about my decision to marry Jo, especially as in some ways I've not just married the girl, but the whole family! My father-in-law is a tremendous role model for me, with his own background in the priesthood and running a business. He's a larger than life character who loves his faith. He's got six children, and a wonderful family, so he's moved on, leaving all the baggage of the seminary behind him. I know that married life can be as onerous and potentially traumatic as monastic life, but I'm better prepared for marriage. I know what I have to do, that I must keep relying on God. In our marriage, God is the third person, an essential part of the Trinity of our relationship. Marriage is the only one of all the sacraments where the two people themselves make the sacrament effective. It is their commitment to one another. You can't do that without God. Looking back, I couldn't have done anything without God. It's been quite a journey, but one in which He's been a constant companion.

'At our wedding, Father David said that I should never feel ashamed of my decision to leave the monastery, because that experience made me the man I am today. All I have learned through it about myself and God will stand me in good stead for the next stage of my life. All I know is that whatever life has in store for me, I'm looking forward to it!'

Declan

It was 2 May 1994, when Declan Murphy's name was splashed across the daily papers and hit television news headlines. All these years later, the sight of the brilliant young jump jockey crumpled and lifeless on the course at Haydock Park with his skull crushed is something that, even now, race-followers, from taxi drivers to housewives, say they'll never forget. And ironically it's a day that Declan himself will never remember...

Twenty-six years earlier, Declan had been born into a large Catholic family near the village of Hospital in County Limerick. His father was a farmer who also ran the waterworks, while his mother had her hands full bringing up five boys and three girls. However, from the very start, there was a bond of closeness between her and her second youngest child, which lasted until her death and beyond. Declan remembers her loving warmth, and the way in which she was quietly able to make an impact on her lively family. He was aware she thought he was different, more complex than her other youngsters. At that time, life in that area of southern Ireland was a simple existence where the Church and the land were the main focal points. Perhaps the 'difference' stemmed from Declan's reaction to the education he received from the Christian Brothers, which he still describes as 'privileged' in spite of its strict discipline enforced by leather straps. 'The nuns instilled principles into my life,' he says. 'My education taught me values. Those principles and values learned from school and from my mother made me what I am today. It would be so much harder to cope without them.'

Many lads in Hospital knew they would grow up to be farmers like their fathers and brothers. Declan was different. He knew farming wasn't for him, and that nothing around him captured his imagination as a possible career. He was simply interested in everything, and his total belief in himself had him trying his hand at anything going. It was that cheeky confidence which almost by accident brought him into the world which subsequently not only gave him a good living, but almost claimed his life.

As Declan grew up in an area renowned for its great hunting tradition, ponies were more accessible to him than bicycles. On Sundays from Easter until the start of October, racetracks would be set up in fields and open spaces across Ireland when people would come from far and wide to watch young lads hurtle round the course on an odd assortment of ponies, going hell for leather, determined to win. Then the winners from each town and district would finally compete countrywide to find the Irish Champion Pony Rider.

Unlike most boys in his neighbourhood, Declan had no interest in ponies. One day, when he was ten years old, Christy Doherty knocked on the door. 'My brother Eamonn was a couple of years older than me,' explains Declan, 'and already established as a good pony rider, whereas I had yet to try it. In spite of the age difference, Eamonn and I looked quite alike – at least, Christy certainly thought so that day! He looked at me and said, "Eamonn, can you come racing down at West Cork on Sunday, and ride my pony at

Inchigeelagh?" So I looked him straight in the eye and replied, "Yes, of course." In fact, I'd never ridden in a pony race in my life before!

'He picked me up as planned on the Sunday – but by the time we got near Inchigeelagh, he'd sussed that I wasn't actually Eamonn at all. "But I can ride as well as Eamonn," was my reply, but he explained that he really couldn't let me race without proper experience, and he'd have to find somebody else. So I was left at the track wandering around when I heard another chap was looking for a rider for a pony in the same race. I found the man, and said, "I'll ride it!" He was a bit doubtful when he realized I was only ten, but he must have been desperate. He soon changed his tune, though, when I not only beat the pony I was supposed to be riding in the first place – but I won!

'That year I made pony racing history. I was only ten and had never ridden in a race before – but by the end of the season I had become champion pony rider for the whole of Ireland.

'Eamonn just laughed when he heard I'd had the gall to pretend I was somebody else. But I suppose I was just lucky, even at that age. I was never intimidated by anything or anybody. I rode for about three years until I got too heavy around the age of thirteen, and I'd made quite a bit of money too – but it didn't really give me the bug for riding. I didn't see it as a career.

'By the time I was sixteen, Eamonn was an apprentice jockey on the Curragh, the Newmarket of Ireland. I went to stay with him during my summer holidays, and his trainer told me he thought I was a very good rider and that I ought to become an amateur jockey. I really wasn't interested – but by the following Monday, he said he'd organized a licence for me, and wanted me to ride for him in a real race at a proper course. I felt very calm because I was just going along with the idea, not intimidated at all – but being competitive is in my nature, I suppose, because I was put in a situation where I had to succeed — and I came in first! It was a big race — and I won on my first ride! Of course, it captured all the headlines because I was still a schoolboy. It had never happened before that the leading amateur jockey in the country was still at school!

'There was quite a lot of pressure on me then to turn professional, but I really didn't want to do that. School was important to me, so I stuck with it, and I suppose it was because I was rather aloof from riding that people wanted me more than ever. When I finally did leave school at eighteen, I had a choice to come to England and ride, or go and study criminal law in the States. I chose the States. Mind you, I managed to fit in a fair amount of riding too, on both sides of the Atlantic, coming back regularly to ride as an amateur for Barney Curley, an interesting man, who encouraged me a lot. After two years, I decided that perhaps I ought to give riding a go by turning professional. By that time, I was riding really good horses and had won the Irish Champion Hurdle, so I was offered the job of first jockey to one of the best yards in the country with the trainer Josh Gifford. Very quickly, over a couple of seasons, I became one of the leading riders on the circuit, winning the Irish Champion Hurdle twice, the Mackeson Gold Cup, the Tripleprint Gold Cup and the Queen Mother Champion Chase. I just gave it all I'd got.

'Mind you, I was riding some great horses by then — Royal Derbi, Deep Sensation, Bradbury Star — I had a great association with all of them. The relationship between horse and jockey is so important, where communication is the secret of success. Mostly I got to know the horses quite well, but occasionally I met my ride for the first time on the day of the race. I remember winning the Tripleprint Gold Cup for the champion trainer Martin Pipe, on a horse called Fragrant Dawn — and the only time I ever sat on that horse was the day I rode him to win.

'People often talk about jump races being particularly dangerous, but danger is how you perceive it. Of course, it's a head-contact sport, and in that respect one of the most perilous – but I always felt totally in control, just as you do if you drive a car on the motorway. You don't think because there has been a sixteen-car pile-up on that stretch of road the week before, the same is going to happen to you. You feel in control of the car you're driving. It's the same with race riding. I never really feared anything at all.

'Three years on, I was still first jockey to Josh Gifford, winning most of the major races I rode in – the Irish Champion Hurdle, the Queen Mother Champion Chase, The Tripleprint Gold Cup, the Mackeson Gold Cup, the Lanzarote Hurdle, the Bula Hurdle. I knew a lot of people thought I'd really arrived, but although I knew I was good, I felt that I was only just starting. There was still room for improvement, and I intended to be better than ever.'

And then it happened – on 2 May 1994. It was the last big race of the season at Haydock Park, near Liverpool, and Declan was there to ride the favourite, Arcot. He'd ridden him once before, and Declan said Arcot tried to kill him then! It was a two-mile hurdle race, and by the time the sixteen riders got to the final quarter mile, fourteen of them were behind Declan. Peter O'Sullivan, the well-known television commentator, who was covering the race that day, said at the time that, 'Arcot was arriving on the scene with Declan Murphy in his customary position – leaving everything to the last minute!' He once likened Declan to Scoby Breasley, the legendary post-war flat jockey who was also known as 'The Head Waiter', because apparently both he and Declan always left their break-through to win until the last moment in the race, knowing exactly where the winning post was.

However, on this particular occasion, tragedy struck at one of the fences. What onlookers didn't know at the time was that as Arcot approached the jump, he broke his pelvis and instead of taking off, simply somersaulted over the fence. Apparently Declan collided with his head as he flew out of his seat, so that he was unconscious before he hit the ground, and dead meat as fourteen other horses galloped over him.

The instant they saw Declan, the paramedics at the course knew he was in trouble. His skull was obviously badly crushed, and frankly they didn't expect him to live. Their reactions were quick, professional and efficient as they put the young rider onto a stretcher, and gave him a drip to keep him alive.

In fact, it wasn't only the paramedics who doubted Declan would pull through. Sky Television announced the news that he actually *was* dead, and all the major broadcasting stations carried footage of the accident. The racing world held its breath as television screens were filled over and over again with the image of Declan tumbling lifeless to the ground with other horses galloping over him. If he wasn't dead, that would be unbelievable enough. For him to recover sufficiently to be anything more than a vegetable would take nothing less than a miracle. Sadly they agreed: Declan Murphy's short and dramatic horse-racing career, like his life, was over.

For a nearly week he lay in a coma. He had known nothing of the dramatic dash by ambulance with police escort from Warrington Hospital to which he had first been taken, to one of the finest senior neurological units in England which was just half an hour away in Walton. He knew nothing of the emergency operation to remove a blood clot from his brain, caused by at least twelve fractures to his skull. He didn't hear the discussion after the operation about the fact that it had been successful as far as anyone knew, but that in order to alleviate the blood clot to the brain, they had had to interfere with the main nerves of the body, and in particular, the optic nerves to the eye. He'd be paralysed almost certainly, and definitely partially blind. Whatever the future held for Declan, it would certainly be limited, requiring tremendous courage and adjustment from a young man who had previously been used to winning every challenge life threw at him.

What Declan does recall from the four days in which he was in a coma is the vivid experience of reliving his childhood. That experience was so real that when he finally emerged to open his eyes and see friends and family around him, he remembered their faces as if from his childhood. Although he knew he recognized them, he couldn't understand the context in which he was seeing them. They looked familiar, and yet nothing was the same. He had no idea why he was in hospital, because he had no recollection of the accident. In his mind, he was a boy of twelve. His later life meant nothing to him. His career as a jockey and the race that had practically claimed his life were simply stories people told him. He didn't remember who he was. He listened to what people told him, but in reality, he remembered nothing – not then, and not now.

'Because I didn't remember what had happened,' says Declan, 'when they first told me I'd be paralysed to some extent, and partially blind too, it meant nothing to me, as if the doctor were speaking to somebody behind me. In fact, that is probably one reason why I recovered as much as I did, because I had such an inner belief that no matter what was said to me, it wouldn't get me down. It wasn't until later, when I'd gone home and a couple of friends came to see me – and I realize now that I was in a pretty bad state, not able to walk and my balance totally gone – that the concern in their faces as they looked at me brought me up short. I couldn't understand why they were speaking to me in such sympathetic tones. They didn't think I would get better! That was such an alien thought to me that from then on, I simply stopped seeing people.

'I had come back home unable to walk, feed myself, get dressed without help, sleep naturally – unable, in fact, to remember who I was. Worst of all was the fact that I had no emotional memory. Thoughts just floated in my head, like pictures with no feelings. In the end, I pieced together an idea of what I was supposed to be from what others told me. It was the most difficult thing I've ever done in my life. In some ways, I am the victim of my own success, in that I camouflaged my lack of memory, giving the impression that I was carrying on with my life as if nothing had happened.

'One odd experience was when I came back home to Newmarket. I had actually bought this house the week before the accident — but afterwards, when I was asked if I still wanted it, I had no idea. I couldn't remember buying it. Finally I decided that if I had wanted it before my fall, then I'd probably want it now — and I have been here ever since. Today I wouldn't part with it for gold. It's me, my home, my safe haven.

'I woke up from the coma to find that I had a very dear girlfriend called Joanna. I didn't know why I recognized her, but I felt as if she were family, and I was immediately comforted by her strength. Joanna was just about the only person who was regularly with me during the months of my recovery. She was fantastic, even gave up her job to take care of me. She shielded me from visitors, and I felt secure with her, because she believed in my strength and determination to get better. Whatever happened, she took it in her stride, never allowing circumstances to affect her belief in me, or my belief in myself. Because of her, I was able to apply myself to the challenge of getting back to normal with every ounce of strength I could muster.

'One day about six weeks after my fall, she was supporting me on one side as I was walking with a stick down a private road, when a car came close to me, and because I couldn't comprehend distance, I really thought it was going to knock me down. I fell down on to the road in a complete state of shock — and once Joanna had managed to get me home in a passing car and called the doctor, I had to be sedated because my whole body was actually vibrating on the bed. That was a real setback, because probably for the first time I began to be aware of the reality of my physical condition. The only way I could get through this was by drawing on my inner strength, my determination to be the "me" I knew I really was. It's not until you have to depend on your inner strength that you realize just how deep those resources can be.

'That inner strength made me determined to push myself much harder than I think I should have done. I wanted to walk. At the time, walking was a huge physical challenge, but I was too defiant to accept that. I remember so clearly one day being taken out into the garden with someone each side of me. I was walking with their support when I asked them to let go of me. They did – and I went down like a brick. I was so angry, beating my walking stick with fury and frustration on the ground, filled with exasperation that I was unable to master something as basic as putting one foot in front of the other. Finally, I calmed down and regained my composure – but my determination was stronger than ever. I was going to walk again, not that day, not until a couple of weeks later, in fact – but walk I did!

'What was really frustrating was the fact that although I was doing everything I could to get physically stronger, the messages being sent by my brain weren't always getting through to parts of my body. For some time I had no feeling in my feet, so walked barefoot rather than acknowledge my paralysis. One day I walked up the road on my own bouncing a golf ball and catching it between different fingers and my thumb as I went, in order to encourage my system to function properly. Suddenly, a car pulled up beside me with two of my friends in it. They were coming to visit me and had stopped to ask for directions. When Colin wound down the window, he went completely pale when he realized it was me, and that I was walking barefoot down the road with my feet completely covered in blood. I had stepped on a broken bottle, and the piece of glass was still sticking out of my foot. I could neither see nor feel it, because I was so focused on the golf ball. I was oblivious to everything – and that was what continued to worry my doctors. At a subconscious level, my body was trying to tell me that I was attempting too much, and it couldn't cope. I simply overrode that, ignoring the signs in my determination to get back to being my normal self.

'I thought about riding. I'd look at pictures of myself winning races, and think, "I'll be there again." It was six months after my accident that I finally sat on a pony, and all my instincts for riding instantly came back to me. The next day I got on to a racehorse. I was a jockey – and even though I had a long way to go, I knew in my own mind that one day I would race again. If I'd mentioned that thought to anyone else, they would have said I was mad. I didn't care. Before my accident, I was a jockey, and a good one. And that was what I would be again, of that I had no doubt. I worked harder than ever to build up my physical strength, spending hours at the gym, and constantly doing exercises to retrain my co-ordination.

'Twelve months from that time when I first sat on a horse again, just a year and a half after my fall, I was back at the racecourse. At Chepstow they have a mile-long race in which flat jockeys challenge jump jockeys. It was a big event, with television coverage and huge crowds and decent prize money at stake, so there was no loyalty between competitors. Your best friend would carve you up on the racetrack. It's like a football game, cut-throat and competitive.

'I remember being really encouraged by the reaction of the crowd. They gave me such a welcome. It was great, although in reality I was completely focused at the time, just concentrating on the job in hand. I made all the running for most of the race, dictating my own pace. I felt I'd got it right – and about halfway through I suddenly realized that I had a chance of winning. The rest of the race is a blur really, until the incredible moment when I actually passed the winning post to be greeted by cheering and applause. I'd won! Whatever I do at any point in the rest of my life, nothing will ever bear comparison to that moment! I was numb to everything except the huge sense of relief that I had actually done it! Eighteen months of determination to overcome all the odds that were stacked against me were realized in one minute thirty-six seconds!

'But after the race, I collapsed in a heap. For a whole week, I was completely exhausted. I slept solidly for days, unable to drag myself out of bed or rise from the chair because I felt so weak. For eighteen months I had focused on that race, and my need to prove myself to everyone who believed in me. Suddenly I'd done it – and I was absolutely washed out. I was twenty-eight years old, with success, disaster and triumph behind me, and an empty page ahead of me.

'Funnily enough, I've never felt bitter about that accident – never thought, "Why me?" Changes in my life have always been dramatic. My accident was about as dramatic as it can get. Most of all, I'd come through, fought my way back and retained my dignity. I had climbed to the top of my mountain and placed a flag upon it. But now it was time to change again. A new direction was needed as I stepped into the next stage of my life.

'I was determined to pick up the strands of my old career, but in my heart I knew that I should not have got my licence to ride back again. It was very clear to me that I wasn't really recovered. I was acting as if nothing had happened, that I hadn't really had my brain torn apart just eighteen months earlier. I had almost become immune to the headaches and pain – at least, I learned to ignore the discomfort. I was wise enough to know, though, that in the competitive field of riding, I would be exposed and vulnerable – and so I decided to walk away.

'In fact, a new career opened up to me almost immediately when I was invited to become a commentator for the Racing Channel. I did that six days a week for two years. At that point, I realized that I had to cut down, and face the fact that I wasn't really recovered at all. I had been dismissing the headaches for so long, but as they intensified and I began to lose my peripheral vision and major senses such as my power of speech, I knew that I finally had to accept that my brain was terribly injured, shutting down on me, giving in.

'As the reality of my injuries hit me, I found it difficult to share that knowledge. I pushed people away, not wanting to let anyone down, or let them know what was happening to me because it felt like an admission of weakness. I didn't want them to think I was in pain, or worry about me.

'I'll never forget sitting down all by myself in the main lounge of this house one evening. The room was dark and it was silent, because light and sound really affected my brain – and for the very first time since my accident I thought the curtains were starting to close on me. At that moment, it seemed to me that the light at the end of the tunnel was in fact an oncoming train. I totally accepted what was happening to me. It didn't frighten me. There was absolutely nothing either I or anyone else could do.

'I was surrounded by friends, but I chose not to involve them in what I was going through. However, one woman, Serena Oxley, who worked as an almoner for the Injured Jockeys' Fund, was a tremendous support to me at that time. She had been visiting me since my accident, but when she came to see me shortly after that evening, I was relieved at the way she understood what the doctors could not understand. I didn't want to be treated as an invalid. She could equate to my whole experience in a language I recognized. She became my listening ear, and I instinctively trusted her. I will always be grateful for the enormous comfort she brought me. She helped me to accept the reality of my physical limitations. With her support, I became even more confident that I had to trust my own instincts about the best way of dealing with my condition, even if it meant disregarding what the doctors were saying about the strong medication I was taking. Drugs were affecting my ability to fight, suppressing my strength. I made the decision that I was more comfortable with a really bad headache, knowing I had one, than being sedated so that I was unaware of the effects of the headache and immune to everything else.

'That was in December 1998 – and I realized that having already climbed to the top of one mountain in regaining enough physical ability to get back on a horse and win a race, I now had a much bigger mountain to climb. The difference was that now I knew how far away the top of the mountain actually was.

'To add to everything I was going through at that time, my mother, who had always been so important to me, was facing a crisis of her own. She had developed motor neurone disease, and was really very seriously ill. It affected me deeply to see her suffer, because of the love I felt for her, and the bond there was between us. She had made me the person I am. She'd never experienced the privileges and good times I'd had, but accepted the very basic pleasures that life brought her. She wanted nothing more, because she was a giving person. She taught me the value of giving, and that has been one of the most essential lessons I have ever learned.

'When I became so ill again myself, I felt I had to hide my condition from her. Of course she was worried, just as any mother would be, especially when she saw in the papers and on television that I had stopped commentating because of a recurrence of my brain injury. I told her that they had got it all wrong – that there was nothing wrong with me, and I just needed a bit of time out to write a book. And because I couldn't bear telling her a lie, I decided to make it the truth. I started a novel then, which has become a real passion for me ever since. I remember taking passages from it to show her now and then. I couldn't bear the thought of her worrying about me, when she had enough to worry about herself. When she finally died, I was bereft. Nothing has ever touched me so intensely. I felt as if I'd lost my security, my whole way of thinking. Even now, I never feel she's far from me. Her gentle strength and influence are with me always.

'Six years on from my accident, I've learned that recovering is accepting my vulnerability. I know I shouldn't carry on living as if I don't have a damaged brain. I've tried to learn to adjust. I still get headaches, although they don't last so long or hurt so badly. I have no on/off switch in my brain, so I need tremendous discipline to sleep naturally, because without sleep my condition becomes more apparent, my concentration falters and the headaches become worse. I won't take pills or medication of any sort for anything. I keep as fit as I possibly can, because I recognize the need for compatibility both mentally and physically. I always treasure something that Mussolini said: "I'd rather live like a lion for a day than a lamb for a lifetime." I'm like that. I don't want to live for ever, but I want to live the life I have to the full.'

To meet Declan today, you soon become aware that running races is so much in his blood that it has become a way of life. For him, there is always a winning line, always a hurdle to face. 'Every day I wake a winner, and only I can make myself a loser. I've come through so much adversity, with a strength and determination to keep me winning. I know that has built me, made me what I am. I simply want to get on with things, be everything that I should be. I don't want to be second best. I am going to live to my utmost until the moment I die. No regrets. No "if only".

'It's instinctive for us to look for reasons why things happen to us, but I've learned to accept that we live our lives in inevitable danger, and that sometimes it's best not to look round corners to try and prejudge what perils lie ahead. If I knew I was going to die tomorrow, I'd just think, "Right, what shall I do tonight?" No one's eternal. We're all just passing through. Perhaps one day, I'll reach a state of contentment – and since my accident, contentment has felt as far away from me as Mars from the world! But finally, after all the adversity I've faced and overcome, contentment seems a real possibility. That would be best of all, and hardest to achieve – but I'll get there, with great thankfulness for all the joy, love, challenge and experience that have made me what I am today.'